WHAT CHURCH LEAD
GROWING CHURCHE
ABOUT *CHURCH GROWTH FLYWHEEL:*

"Rich is right again. Momentum is hard to catch, easy to lose, and most important. If Flywheel has any importance, it has loads of importance. Don't miss this book!"

CLAY SCROGGINS, LEAD PASTOR, NORTH POINT COMMUNITY CHURCH

"Rich Birch has knocked it out of the park with *Church Growth Flywheel*. His new book is full of practical helps for church leaders looking to reach more people in their communities. Rich cuts through the theory and offers solid advice and guidance that you can put into action right away."

DAN REILAND, EXECUTIVE PASTOR, 12STONE CHURCH, LAWRENCEVILLE, GEORGIA

"Thank you Rich, for pouring your years of experience and research into this helpful resource. I'm so grateful for this one-stop-shopping tool designed to help more churches reach more people with the good news of Jesus. "

BRUXY CAVEY, AUTHOR OF (RE)UNION AND THE END OF RELIGION, TEACHING PASTOR AT THE MEETING HOUSE

"Rich Birch has been reading my mind! After reading the first 15 pages, I made this book mandatory reading for my entire staff."

HAL SEED, CHIEF MENTOR AT PASTORMENTOR.COM AND FOUNDING PASTOR OF NEW SONG COMMUNITY CHURCH

"Rich is one of my top 3 "go-to guys" for identifying strategies that actually move the ball up the field when it comes to connecting people to our churches. This book is an engaging step by step guide that does just that: It's simple, compelling and doable. Read it with your calendar open. "

"What an incredible book! Rich has a unique way of sharing real and relevant practices from his experience and conversations that will no doubt be a game changer for you and your church community. *Church Growth Flywheel* is a gift to church leaders filled with practical yet challenging steps to help initiate growth and change within your community. And what church leader doesn't want to see more lives changed by Christ!"

"In *Church Growth Flywheel*, Rich helps us as leaders think through the way we lead our churches, understand the dynamics of how our churches are perceived in today's world and for us all to become futurists in painting a landscape for that allows us to have Kingdom impact for the gospel message. Thanks for making us think about how we impact the world Rich...well done!"

"Rich has done another outstanding job of laying out very simple and practical ways you can reach more people, faster. *Church Growth Flywheel* is a must for any church leader who wants to get more people in the door of their church so they can hear the Good News of Jesus."

"This book is a MUST READ for every leader with a desire to see their church reach its full redemptive potential and connect as many people as possible to Jesus. Rich is refreshingly pragmatic so if you've ever been frustrated and thought, "Yeah, but HOW?..." this is the book for you.

When it comes to church growth, Rich isn't one who merely speculates. He's a student and practitioner who has done us all a favor by documenting what he's learned from the network of leaders he has interviewed and his own leadership experience. Read and then be bold enough to apply what you'll learn from this book and the results will make you glad you did."

KENT JACOBS, LEAD PASTOR | EPIC CHURCH

"If you have any intention to grow you need to read this book. Rich does an incredible job of taking the mystery out of how you can grow! I wish I had this resource as a new leader."

STEPHEN BREWSTER, EXECUTIVE CREATIVE PASTOR OF FREEDOM HOUSE CHURCH

"We are all looking for proven principles of what works in ministry! Rich Birch has laid out some amazing principles in his new book *Church Growth Flywheel*. From his seat as a leader in some of the best churches out there to his work with the unSeminary Podcast and asking great questions from leading churches, he has synthesized the information into this game-changing book! If you are going to lead for the marathon not just the sprint, these flywheel principles will be key!!! Thanks Rich for this leadership gold!!!"

MIKE LINCH, SENIOR PASTOR NORTHSTAR CHURCH (GA), HOST OF THE LINCH WITH A LEADER PODCAST

"In a season when churches are struggling, there's one thing most leaders are trying to regain - MOMENTUM! In *Church Growth Flywheel*, your team will learn how to create momentum around many things you are currently doing at your church - the things you've been doing without purpose or intentionality. If your team is willing to do the hard work towards creating momentum, Church Growth Flywheel should be your handbook!"

DR. JOSH WHITEHEAD, EXECUTIVE PASTOR OF FAITH PROMISE CHURCH

"This came at a great time for our church! I'm endorsing this book, because it legitimately helped our church. The questions we are asking Rich answers. It will help your church also."

RON EDMONDSON, PASTOR - AUTHOR OF THE MYTHICAL LEADER

"Rich is a next-level practitioner of church growth in every sense of the word. When 94% of churches are losing ground in their communities, it's clear that churches need a clear growth strategy if we're going to have any chance of changing the tide. Reading this book is the equivalent of hiring Rich to develop your church growth strategy and gives you the opportunity to draw on his depth of experience to help you engage your community, bless your church and advance God's kingdom."

DAN ZIMBARDI, EXECUTIVE PASTOR OF SANDALS CHURCH

"As a Church Planter, I know all too well that ministry momentum is hard to build and even harder to sustain. The practical ideas and plans laid out by Rich in *Church Growth Flywheel* are both incredibly inspiring and also simple enough to add to our organizational rhythm.

Don't wait till you are 'just a little bit bigger' before implementing these strategies. Rich breaks down a complicated thought into simple and practical steps for any church, no matter the size, to see significant growth."

PETER GOWESKY, LEAD PASTOR, HOPE CITY CHURCH

"If you're looking for new ways to impact your community, breakthrough growth barriers and transform your church, THIS BOOK IS FOR YOU! Its practical and easy to implement strategies will not only help you reach and keep people, but will create the kind of excitement and momentum that leads to radical growth!"

CHRISTINE KREISHER, EXEC. DIR. OF MINISTRIES AT GT CHURCH & AUTHOR OF THE VOLUNTEER PROJECT: STOP RECRUITING. START RETAINING

WHAT THOUGHT LEADERS ARE SAYING ABOUT *CHURCH GROWTH FLYWHEEL:*

"Rich brings a wealth of passion, knowledge and experience to the subject of church growth. He presents a treasure trove of best practices and learnings around engaging people in your city with the message of Christ. *Church Growth Flywheel* is full practical steps that you can actually start doing and growing in your church, today. I'm so grateful for Rich's voice on this subject and I think you will be too."

CAREY NIEUWHOF, FOUNDING & TEACHING PASTOR, CONNEXUS CHURCH

"I've followed Rich Birch for many years as he has had a front row seat to some of the fastest-growing churches in North America. That's why I got excited when I heard he was releasing a book with some of what he has learned. You will be energized, informed, inspired, and equipped after reading *Church Growth Flywheel*."

TIM STEVENS, VICE PRESIDENT OF CONSULTING, VANDERBLOEMEN SEARCH GROUP

"Insanely practical... super simple... and absolutely essential! Rich Birch has captured the disciplines and behaviors that will allow your church to experience growth that enables you to thrive. Buy one for every member of your team and read it together!"

JENNI CATRON, FOUNDER/CEO THE 4SIGHT GROUP AND AUTHOR OF THE 4 DIMENSIONS OF EXTRAORDINARY LEADERSHIP

"In this book, *Church Growth Flywheel*, Rich has distilled years of experience and study to help church leaders succeed. This book is full of practical insights and shortcuts for leaders like you. Worth picking up!"

BRAD LOMENICK, FOUNDER, BLINC; AUTHOR, H3
LEADERSHIP & THE CATALYST LEADER

"Most pastors I meet are frustrated since they are trying tons of tactics for growth, but not seeing any results. It isn't good enough to just go out and just do 100 things. Rich's system is what they are lacking. For sustained growth, you need an end to end process that's strategic and easy to follow. This book gives you the entire blueprint in one shot."

KENNY JAHNG, FOUNDER, CHURCH BUTLER SOCIAL MEDIA

"What makes *Church Growth Flywheel* a must read is that is a book with practical applications. Rich is not just a theorist of church growth, multiplication and reaching people for the gospel...he is a Practitioner. He has lived it. He has led it. He has gotten his hands dirty DOING IT! As Rich says..."We need your church to grow. We need your church to make a difference." We are counting on you!"

TIM COOL, CHIEF SOLUTIONS OFFICER, COOL SOLUTIONS
GROUP

"Rich gives us strategic rocket fuel for growth in our ministries. This book goes way beyond theory and gets practical about what you can do this year to impact your community."

FRANK BEALER, CEO, PHASE FAMILY CENTER / EXECUTIVE
DIRECTOR OF LEADERSHIP DEVELOPMENT AT ORANGE

"Rich is one of the best communicators—and this book proves it. It's full of practical ideas for church growth during "such a time as this.""

KATIE ALLRED, CHURCHCOMMUNICATIONS.COM
CO-FOUNDER

"Rich Birch is in the unique position to hear from a large number and a wide range of church leaders. As a result, this book serves as a clearinghouse for ideas regarding how churches can best reach their communities. Given the statistic Rich sites that 94% of all the churches in America are losing ground in their communities, the practical systems he shares are very much needed!"

LEE KRICHER, AUTHOR, FOR A NEW GENERATION: A
PRACTICAL GUIDE FOR REVITALIZING YOUR CHURCH

"Rich Birch is passionate about growing local churches and he is no armchair cheerleader. He's a seasoned and winsome practitioner who's been in the trenches of three growing churches and has helped numerous other churches to grow across Canada and the United States. He unashamedly believes churches are designed to grow and his book *"Church Growth Flywheel: 5 Practical Systems to Drive Growth At Your Church"* is an easy, quick read with practical and proven best practices. Implement these systems and get your church flywheel rolling!"

JIM TOMBERLIN PASTOR, AUTHOR, FOUNDER & PRESIDENT
OF MULTISITE SOLUTIONS

"This book is a regular must-read on my bookshelf. I love Rich's "Five Spokes of the *Church Growth Flywheel*." It is so true what he says 'If you pull out one of the spokes from a five-spoke wheel, the tire will go flat on one side.' I need to annually review the "flywheel" to ensure that I haven't missed one of his spokes. Pure genius! How can I influence church growth ... ensure that all the spokes are working!"

DAVID FLETCHER, EXECUTIVE PASTOR AND FOUNDER OF
XPASTOR.ORG

"Execution. This book is all about getting things done in a way that will help you reach your community for Christ. Rich has wonderfully weaved stories and principles in a way that will lead you to action. Don't miss this incredibly practical book."

DANIEL IM, AUTHOR OF NO SILVER BULLETS, COAUTHOR OF PLANTING MISSIONAL CHURCHES, DIRECTOR OF CHURCH MULTIPLICATION AT NEWCHURCHES.COM, AND TEACHING PASTOR

CHURCH GROWTH FLYWHEEL

5 PRACTICAL SYSTEMS **TO DRIVE GROWTH** AT YOUR CHURCH

RICH BIRCH
Foreword by Carl F. George

To **my dad**, Larry Birch

*Seeing **Jesus' impact** your life upclose has been one of the greatest joys of my life.*

*The fact that you still get **misty eyed** when talking about how the **church** should be **reaching people** far from God is a part of the **passion behind this book**.*

TABLE OF
CONTENTS

FOREWORD

YOU ARE IN for a fun reading experience. This book stimulates appetite for innovation. It brings thrilling stories of success from churches where positive changes are happening and shows where to start in bringing about such results where you are.

Rich Birch invited my collaborator Warren Bird and me to come on his podcast[1]. We were introducing a current release of our book, *How to Break Growth Barriers: Revise Your Role, Release Your People, and Capture Overlooked Opportunities for Your Church*[2]. The podcast experience was delightful. Rich has a

---

1 Rich here...I loved having them on the podcast. You can hear that episode at this link: http://bit.ly/cgf_carl
2 This is a must read from my perspective. It pairs well with this book! ;) http://bit.ly/cgf_barriers

style that sparkles and brings an uplifting emotion to any discussion.

Rich has ministered in large, fast growing churches. He shares many attractive ideas on how to improve the reach and connecting power of the churches of today. I am impressed with the powerful examples and arguments he brings to this discussion. It is a short book, a quick read, but packs enormous power for inspiring action.

Pastors spend years in serious studies to equip themselves with the arguments that satisfy curious minds and hearts. Their orthodoxy is assured by thorough attention to the great classics and the faith. They are introduced to the great ideas and doctrines that have guided the church through the centuries. They even train in sermon preparation and delivery, and in how to conduct rituals and give one on one counsel. In courses on pastoral theology, they receive what carries them through weddings and funerals. What many of them realize later on is that the governance and organizational development work required for successfully leading a congregation to expansion is not covered as well as it might be.

Rich has noted this lack of practical organizational leadership knowledge in his slogan: *stuff you wish they taught you seminary.* My career at Fuller in Pasadena was focused predominantly on the mid-career pastor. As pastors returned for D.Min. programs, most were veterans with a decade of experience and a keenly felt desire to learn what they had not previously been given. Many of those with whom I worked confessed that they were not ready to hear, during their seminary years, what they now eagerly studied with us. We were making available then what I see Rich Birch bring in his book and podcasts: help for leading and managing their congregations as they reach out to touch people beyond their members.

The flywheel analogy is a compelling one. It highlights the role of momentum in making changes. At first, inertia works against change, but then realigns expectations that help facilitate more and more changes. In the years that I have been consulting churches, a three year cycle has been apparent. Sadly, many leaders put their whole heart into making changes for a year or two, then tire of the effort and stand back, out of breath, for the next season, when they would have been able to see the results of their dreams had they persisted to a breakout. Success breeds success, and a small success can encourage a leader or a group to attempt even greater things as they move forward.

Rallying people to a cause and creating a sense of celebration helps everyone focus on an objective. Old Testament Israel was given a calendar of days to gather and celebrate. Several times each year, the people were summoned to participate in times of rejoicing, some solemn and some festive. Even merchants promote their wares and services by seasonal sales and special offers. Church members that are pulled together to promote good works that everyone in their community can see as helpful will reap emotional benefits from the goodwill they show. The principle is simple. The congregations that practice this principle benefit greatly from it.

Older readers will readily admit to their bewilderment with aspects of the digital economy. Every segment of their lives is impacted as result of changes in technology. How we learn, communicate, shop, bank, war, travel, eat, worship, and even protect our young, are all affected. Ours is a time of profound change, and churches are not immune from it. However what Rich shares in this work, which includes a good working understanding of the digital world, is more necessary and more needed than a digital makeover for a church.

Churches are uniquely poised to have impact in their communities, because they are in possession of themselves. They represent a body of talent and energy and money that is already present. Churches resemble fully assembled automobiles that sit idling their engines, but not moving. What spark or insight can summon those resources and release them to the benefit of those in need? How does a leader stimulate sleeping people and get them moving into an effective rescue force?

Change is hard, as inertia must be overcome by the persistent application of great energy. What will it take to move beyond where we have been? What is the new ground that will mobilize members and excite communities? Rich reports from the front lines how community engagement stimulates members and can result in strangers and outsiders inquiring about what you are up to and why.

Instead of bewailing the injustice and poverty within our ministry areas, Rich urges us to examine the needs so abundantly present and challenge those needs with concrete expressions of love. He urges us to embrace the mobilization of our people to the benefit of others as seminal to changing the growth climate of our congregations. Human neediness is apparent everywhere. Our churches have volunteer resources available within them that are largely untapped. Enthusiastic challenges to our members which lead to helping those in need are the starting place for a radical shift in how our churches are perceived by unchurched people. It creates an atmosphere of approval in a community towards the church and opens it to inquirers.

Promoting positive changes in a congregation is a continual work. By addressing the work to be done topically, in five phases, effort can be concentrated for immediate impact. Rich promotes making the most of immediately implementable changes that can accumulate into an environment in which people can help other people feel a part of a larger, more embracing whole. It is community building for today, and a promising path toward the future.

Carl F. George
Greenville, SC

INTRODUCTION
(to my bias)

WHENEVER I FIND an opportunity to meet with any church leaders in small groups of less than 50 people, I always ask a simple question: "*What was your favorite burger joint when you were a kid? You know, the one that served the burger that you still think about, even as an adult. Tell me about that place.*"

Well, now you too, are thinking about it, aren't you? It's okay—go ahead, take a moment and cherish your own favorite burger spot from your childhood, which holds a special place in your heart and which, you make a point to visit, whenever you're in town.

Everybody always has a ready response to this question, and it poses as a great conversation starter: they give me their names, and they inevitably tell me a little about themselves. That way, with just one question, I learn where they're from, maybe where they've travelled, and a bit about their families.

Of course, people talk about the most obscure places. I often hear about a mom-and-pop shop that makes "the most amazing burger," the kind that initiates cravings for it just by thinking about it, the kind that makes you want to drive for miles just to have a quick bite.

These stories always take me back to Weber's on Highway 11, heading out of Toronto, Ontario, where I grew up. I can never forget this little hangout situated on the side of the highway, which could be seen while heading into cottage country. Here, people would stop along the way to their vacation destinations or to the summer camps where they'd be dropping off the kids. For me, and for thousands of others, grabbing a burger at Weber's was a much-anticipated summer ritual. Even to this day, people stop there by the thousands. They don't seem to mind the summer sun beating down on their shoulders as they sweat it out, waiting in the queue just to buy a simple cheeseburger from Weber's menu—they don't offer many toppings or much of what we'd term as variety. (They do offer a very good chocolate milkshake, though.)

Sometimes, the folks mention something like The Varsity in downtown Atlanta, Georgia (which is technically more of a hot dog place). This is a great stop, and the fans maintain that classic food, retro-style paper hats, and orange drinks along with the one-of-a-kind ordering experience, which is well worth the effort and time spent finding a parking spot (Don't forget to pick up one of those little paper hats for the kids!)

Lately, though, I have been hearing more and more people talking about the hip indie eateries popping up around the country, like The Burgers Priest, which has cloaked everything from its marketing to the menu options in a religious iconography. Just imagine putting in this order: *"A Tower of Babel and Armageddon, please."*

Do you know which restaurant I hear about very rarely? Yes, you guessed it: McDonald's. It's ironic that a very few people rave about the Big Mac, especially when you take into consideration the fact that McDonald's sells way more hamburgers than all these other burger places put together and continues to be a dominant force in terms of hamburger sales around the world. They *are* the real burger king (apologies to that other restaurant).[3]

WHAT'S A BURGER GOT TO DO, GOT TO DO WITH IT?

By now, you are definitely wondering why on earth this dude is spending so much time talking about burgers if this is, in fact, a book about church growth. I mean,

---

3 Crazy, right! Here's a fun fact: McDonald's could lose 50% of its sales and still end up in first place in the burger selling business! http://bit.ly/cgf_mcdee

sure, I have used that question frequently enough to the point that it's become my favorite icebreaker, but I'll go ahead and admit that it's a bit of a set-up, too.

I'm talking burgers because I want you to understand my bias.

Yes, I have a bias. In fact, we all do—and it's not a dirty word; it's not even a terrible thing. However, it *is* something you should be aware of before we move forward together in this book. You and I are going to be spending a lot of time together talking about your church and so, I want you to understand where I'm coming from. It's important for me to share with you the way I think about and approach the following things:

- our churches;

- what God has called us to do;

- our responsibility to reach the communities that God has placed us in.

So what does my bias exactly have to do with burgers?

Before I answer that, we need to go back to McDonald's just for a second.

You can go anywhere in America, into any town - large and small alike, and on the main drag, usually the busiest place in town, you'll find a McDonald's. Recently, a McDonald's opened up on the two corners of a concession in the countryside, along a road that I drive on quite often. I am still amazed that every time I drive by, no matter the time of day or year, there are at least half a dozen people waiting in the drive through there. There are *always* people waiting in the queue. McDonald's has been able to scale both the ubiquity and convenience, ultimately making an impact on all the customers across the country.

My bias is this: I want your church to be more like McDonald's and less like the hip, artisanal-pressed ground beef patty joint. I want your church to be the kind of place where people come and line up to see amazing things happen—not because you've got an amazing burger to sell, but because you've got the most amazing story to tell.

I do realize that comparing your church to McDonald's may have already caused some of you to get in your car as quickly as you can say McNugget, roll down your windows, and hurl this book at the first Mickey D's that you pass as you continue driving towards your nearest obscure burger restaurant for a bison-avocado-chipotle patty melt.

I get it—there are plenty of people out there who just can't stand McDonald's, and not just because they skimp on the beef or because of the forever-broken ice-cream machines. For many, McDonald's represents the commercial excess in America. If that's the case, feel free to stop thinking about the golden arches and substitute it with your favorite coffee shop into this analogy. The college hangout, the hole-in-the-wall where the old-timers have their morning cuppa, the diner around the corner—whatever you choose, for it resonates with you for a variety of reasons. Would you claim a mega-chain as your all-time favorite coffee shop? Starbucks dominates the top-java category - a feat that very few other companies have ever achieved before. Or consider the impact that Dunkin Donuts has had on the country: America really does run on Dunkin!

The analogy even applies to the entertainment franchises. "Tell me about your favorite independent film producer," you inquire, and you'll hear about all kinds of interesting films that you've never heard of before. Imagine the reaction when I reveal that my favorite independent film producer has always been George Lucas.[4] The Star Wars franchise is entering its fourth decade and it's *still* showing all signs of making an impact.

McDonald's, Starbucks, Star Wars—they've all succeeded substantially and still continue gaining traction.

Did you know that the same could happen for your church?

You see, I want your church to succeed because 94% of all the churches in America are losing ground in their communities. [5]

---

4 Yes! George Lucas was an indie filmmaker. In fact, it's a part of what made Star Wars such a powerful brand because he rejected the traditional thinking about producing movies! http://bit.ly/cgf_lucas

5 Another way to say this is that in 2050, the percentage of the US population attending church will be half of what it was in 1990! Those the years that I'm serving in leadership in the local church. We need to turn this around! http://bit.ly/cgf_94

We need your church to grow.

We need your church to make a difference.

I'm a part of that generation of leaders that has seen the Bride of Christ become anaemic and weak, even as we continue in service. I'm hoping that this book would serve as a clarion call. I am aware that that's a high standard. Nevertheless, what I'm hoping it to do is motivate you to think differently, and more importantly, to *act* differently when it comes to church growth. I want to motivate you to do something different by the time you're finished reading this book; I want you to reach out and find newer ways in which you can impact your community. It is my sincere hope that this book serves as a manifesto for radical growth and changes in your church.

I want to challenge you to take a look at the McDonald's in your community—literally, glance over at it every time you pass it from here on out. I guarantee that you'll see people in line inside and lined up in the drive-thru every time—*and that is exactly what I'm hoping will happen for your church.* I want your church not to just be bigger for the sake of being large, but also to have a big influence and big impact on your community. I want to see the big influence. I know that large churches can simply do things on a scale that small churches cannot do.[6]

---

6 This is an oldie but a goodie on the discussion of very large churches and what they provide for communities. http://bit.ly/cgf_edu

THIS BOOK MIGHT NOT BE FOR YOU

Many church leaders are going to dislike this book. There are people who have already put this book back on the shelf or returned it to Amazon thinking that it would be a waste of time for them to read it, and here's why:

1. If you are uncomfortable with the idea of reaching people for the message of Jesus, then this book is not for you.

There are many in the ministry leadership who do not want to reach new people.

It seems hard to believe that anyone would find outreach and sharing the gospel to be a 'bad thing,' but there are church leaders out there who legitimately wonder if they're supposed to reach out and draw new members into the community versus staying put and caring for the small flock that's already in their building. Church leaders who are more interested in keeping than reaching definitely won't like this book.

2. If you're looking for theological discussions around church growth, this book will leave you wanting more.

I know there are church leaders who look at a small group of people gathered inside their building and somehow make an unspoken value judgment that says, *smaller is better than bigger.* If you're a leader of that kind, you're just simply not going to like this book. In fact, I'm convinced that theological wrangling over this topic isn't what church leaders need to do with their time. What we need instead is *more action*, not more reflection to make a difference in our communities.

3. If you read the Scriptures and cannot see that the entire Book tells one story of a God who is so desperately in love with humanity that He pursues them relentlessly, then this book will be of no use to you.

SO, WHO IS THE PERFECT READER OF THIS BOOK, THEN?

This book is for church leaders who look out and wonder, *how are we going to see more people connected to the incredible timeless teaching of Jesus, and to help that teaching make a difference in the lives of the people?* I hope that this book would push you to do things beyond your comfort zone and take you to a place where you're going to think about trying something different simply because you have developed a deep desire to reach people with the message of Jesus.

There are a few things that I need to do throughout these chapters in order to help you propel your church forward:

1. I want to apply personal lessons that I've seen inside some of the fastest-growing churches in the country.

Over the last 20 years, I've had a few opportunities to work with a number of churches that have, collectively, grown close by 350%. That's *three and half times their initial size* from the time I started working with those churches.[7] My experience comes not as a theoretician, but as a practitioner of church growth; it doesn't come from some academic perch, it comes from the authentic, inside-the-ministry application of these practices. I want to help you apply these lessons to your church and give you the confidence, instruction, and tactics in order to ensure that the same things happen in your church.

2. I want to give you an inside look at what more than 200 fast-growing churches.

Over the last several years, I've hosted a weekly podcast called unSeminary[8]. Every week, we interview church leaders from some of the fastest-growing churches in the country. I've only really been talking to churches that have been experiencing growth beyond

---

7 The combined attendance of The Meeting House, Connexus Church, & Liquid Church was somewhere around 2,700 when I started working at those churches. By the time I had finished working with those churches, the combined attendance was somewhere around 9,250. That's a lot of people. Obviously, I'm not saying that I was the growth engine for these churches; I'm saying I had a front row seat to see this growth happen.

8 unSeminary...stuff you wish they taught in seminary! Check it out: www.unseminary.com

what other normal churches experience. In many ways, this book serves as the culmination of hundreds of hours of listening to church leaders and probing to understand what's happening at their churches.

3. I want to push you to take action on this blueprint.

This book doesn't exist merely to share the ideas left untried; on the contrary, the very reason I've written this book is to share new ideas and new strategies that you can take with you into your own church and see the transformation.

Whenever I take a new leader or my team to conferences, I ask them to do just one thing, and I'm going to ask you to the same of you as you read this book: find *one piece* of advice that you can put into action at your church *this month*.

That's right: *this very month.*

Not next year.

Not after Lent.

Not when people are heading home from summer vacation.

This month.

When you're done reading this book, find one idea or strategy, apply it, and see what God can do.

I'm honored in the fact that you would take time to read this book. I know there's a lot that you could be doing with your time, and not only does it honor me, but it also honors your people, too, for you to become a stronger leader, to invest time to find a new way for your church, and to consider how to reach people who currently aren't at your church. Thank you for investing this time.

CHAPTER 1:

YOU NEED A FLYWHEEL

fly·wheel
ˈflī,(h)wēl
noun
a heavy revolving wheel in a machine that is used to increase the machine's momentum and thereby provide greater stability[9].

---

9 I know I'm supposed to show my sources…but this definition just came from Google and they didn't reference where they got it from…so I'll risk it.

DO YOU REMEMBER the merry-go-round at the park you played in when you were a kid? The one that was some combination of a flat piece of steel with giant handlebars around it? It was so heavy, you could hold on to one of the handlebars while keeping one foot up on the platform and the other on the ground.

You had to use all of the energy of your entire leg in an extended position and you would push with every bit of strength that your Osh Kosh B'gosh-sized muscles had—and all this for what? Just to get it to move.

You'd push a little bit harder, and then you'd get a spin.

On the second turn, you had to push almost as hard as the first—but just a *little* bit less.

You still pushed the third time around, and by that time, you thought you'd suddenly gotten as strong as your big sister since you didn't have to use quite as much power.

Then, it was glorious: you would keep pushing until you went from pushing hard to hardly pushing. In fact, in just a matter of a few minutes, you'd generated so much momentum on that merry-go-round that you had to hold on, literally, for dear life.

In many ways, the merry-go-round is like a giant flywheel. If you've never heard of it before, a flywheel is essentially a speed-regulating device that requires momentum in order to keep the engine moving. It's a huge, heavy wheel that requires a large amount of energy on the first push in order for it to get moving. As you push it more, the weight of the wheel takes over and propels you forward—just like on the merry-go-round. Among other commonalities, both of these spinning devices require some amount of momentum—and so does your church.

MOMENTUM: KEEP ON KEEPIN' ON

Momentum is a precious commodity for your church and also for you as a leader. As church leaders—and church members, in fact—we must learn to nurture it. That's a part of the job: to nurture momentum in the body.

1. In order to nurture it, you first have to gain it.

2. Once you gain it, you must capture it.

3. Once you capture it, you have to push towards it and harness it.

4. *Then and only then,* you can nurture it.[10]

In our churches, when we push long enough in a focused direction, we eventually behave as if we're kids on the merry-go-round who go from pushing hard to hardly pushing. Often times, people will look at a growing church, and wonder *what's making that church over there grow so quickly*? Churches grow because their leaders and members put in a lot of effort, and the energy is thus applied in the same direction over an extended period.

I want you to think about this book as a guide to all of the phases of the church growth flywheel: everything in this book works together as one unit pushing towards what it is that God is calling your church to do. Of course, it's going to be a little difficult to learn a new approach at the very beginning. That's a guarantee. Just remember that flywheel, that merry-go-round: *at first, it's a lot of work, but it gets easier over time.*

---

10 Eventually, the momentum of a growing and healthy church gets to the point where you're just holding on! That's a fun stage…a rush…it's really is something amazing to be a part of.

SET LOW EXPECTATIONS
(YES, I REALLY JUST SAID THAT)

What I need you to do is to calibrate your expectations regarding the work that you're about to go into. What you're about to embark on is, frankly, just a lot of work; so fuel up on the Word, the Spirit, and some java because it's going to take long days of work—and maybe some hard nights too—to make things happen in your church.

Lower your expectations for the early results. In the first few months, maybe even in the first few years, change will take place incrementally. Some of the strategies that we're going to talk about are going to take months of labor before you can see the impact that your church is capable of creating.

How long will it take?

1. Maybe 36 months;

2. Three years;

3. 1,000 days[11];

4. However long it takes.

I hope your answer was D because what I am offering you is not a quick approach. This title of this book isn't "The Fast Track" because the fast track doesn't exist.

---

11 I thought about calling this book "1,000 Days to Church Growth," but I don't think you'd have picked it up then. Well, you'd pick it up but not some of the other church leaders. ;)

These strategies are not the Miracle-Gro of method-ologies, but that God blesses our efforts, our energy, and our hearts for Him and His people is some kind of miracle for sure. I am not promising simple ease or a short-term difference. What we're talking about doing is pushing in the same direction over time in order to help your church grow.

BIGGER AND BETTER

Early on in my freshman year of high school, our youth pastor gathered us together in the gym and said, "Tonight, we're going to play a game called Bigger and Better." We divided into groups of half a dozen people, and our leader handed out one paper clip to every small group. He said: "Tonight, we're going to go door-to-door to homes in our community. You'll knock and tell the person at the door that you're from the local church youth group and that we're out tonight. Tell them that you're wondering if they can trade you something for that paperclip, something that's bigger and better. If they say yes, then you take that bigger or better thing and say thank you, and that you are glad for that. If they say no, you say, hey, I still really appreciate this."[12] Reflecting back on that memory, I am sure our youth pastor's goal was that we'd just have

---

12 Sidenote: this is a terrible way to do community engagement. Please don't play this game in your community. It's actually a way to annoy your neighbors.

a fun evening together out in our neighborhood, but I was left with a lifelong leadership lesson.

The results were interesting: sometimes we would go door-to-door and the people wouldn't *quite* slam the door in our faces—but it was very close to that. Sometimes they'd sigh and say, "Oh, actually, now that you do say that, I've got something I would like to give you." Sometimes we'd ask the question, and they would almost immediately say, "Absolutely! I've got something bigger and better for you!" As we'd collect new items, we'd go door-to-door, with a progression in our search for something bigger and better as we passed the time:

- The paperclip would become a pencil.

- The pencil would become a notepad.

- The notepad would become a small coffee table.

- The coffee table would become a couch.
    (I know it seems crazy that in a matter of 90 minutes, one can turn a paperclip into a couch, but that's actually what one of the groups did. They came back 90 minutes later with a couch that they proudly carried it on their shoulders into our youth room and dropped it in there).[13]

---

13 That couch was still there when I graduated from high school four years later. Again, another reason not to do this event. Did you hear about the guy who traded a paperclip for a house? True story...check it out here: http://bit.ly/cgf_bigger

Church growth works the same way as that silly game: you need to stick with these practices time in and time out, regardless of the results. Sometimes, you'll apply some energy and effort and witness short seasons and spurts of growth.

When I was involved with The Meeting House, we dedicated ourselves to implementing a variety of these and such strategies, and there was one weekend during that time where we had as much as 500 new people show up (and stay). Growth may take place incrementally, or it may happen in seasons; there are times you'll go through seasons where it's flat-lined, but like those kids playing Bigger and Better, we need to stick with the strategy because we know we will eventually be able to obtain a better result.

THE FIVE SPOKES OF THE CHURCH GROWTH FLYWHEEL

If you pull out one of the spokes from a five-spoke wheel, the tire will go flat on one side. Sure, the car will still move, but it's definitely not going to propel you forward like the way it would have, had all the spokes been intact.

In this book, we're going to cover five critical components of the church growth flywheel. I'll outline each particular aspect, dive into the tactics, and give you real-life examples of churches that are applying this in their communities. I believe this will inspire you enough to consider how you can initiate growth and change within your own community. You'll also find a series of questions at the end of each chapter that you can use for your team and stir the conversation.

1. Big Days

Don't worry; I'm not going to ask you to have live camels at your Christmas Eve services or to have a robotic Jesus that goes up into the ceiling of your church at Easter. I *am* going to push you to think about how you can make those services and a few others during the year the kind of service, which your people would want to invite their friends to witness, and moreover, which their friends will actually attend.

In this section, we're going to talk about the three or four Sundays which happen at your church every year, and which are critical for the long-term growth of your community. You know those Sundays: the mornings when your people are more inclined towards inviting their friends to come to a service (and their friends are more than willing to attend). We need to ensure that we're crafting experiences on those big days that are set up to encourage invitation, especially to those who may have never attended the church before. You'll learn about how early on in my career, I held convictions and led in a way that hindsight shows actually hindered our ability to reach out to the people with the message of Jesus. We're also going to talk about how churches get visitors from these Big Days to return for all the other days because you might be able to drive in a big audience on Christmas and Easter, but how can you drive them back on non-holidays as well?

2. Series Roll Outs

Your church should be packaging up the way it talks about scripture into series. These stretches of four to eight weeks are the ways to focus on your audience and your community on what it is that you're talking about the teachings of Jesus and the Bible. We all know that people don't just want to know what's on the TV; they want to know what *else* is on TV. This has only become a stronger reality as we now live in a universe influenced by Netflix. How are our churches leveraging the way we talk about our content to help the people wrestle through not only what we're talking about now, but also to make them realize them what we need to be talking about in the future?

3. Content and Social

How can you produce engaging content that can help your community, and how can you leverage social media channels to spread that content?

I don't think your church needs a specific social media strategy for a particular social network. I am aware this might seem controversial in an age where Facebook is so incredibly dominant in most of our lives. However, what I do believe your church needs are a content marketing and social media strategy. We're going to give you action plans for how you can leverage both content and social media channels to drive interest and engagement at your church that ultimately translates not into more likes, comments, and shares, but into driving more people showing up to your services and eventually, drives people to engage in your community.

4. Community Engagement

People want to make a difference in the world. We think it's a God thing, they think it's a good thing. Let's stop fighting them over it, and just work together. I have seen that community engagement is a vitally important tool for church growth as we go into the future and look to reach people that currently aren't in our churches.

Over the last 15 years, we've seen an increasing trend that shows people are more likely to join the church to make a positive social difference in their community before they come to our Sunday morning services. Rather than pushing back on this trend and saying that your church isn't involved in social justice issues, I want you to consider how you can encourage your community to work together for improvement and ultimately see that as a front door for people connecting with your broader church community, including the Sunday morning attendance.

5. Internal Communication

Finally, we'll talk about how you can get your people who are currently in your church the right message at the right time so that they're able to tell their friends everything that's happening at your church and arouse their interests to ultimately get them plugged in. We know that not everyone in your church is inviting their friends to come visit every Sunday, and so in this section, we're going to show you how to identify those audiences who are currently attending on a regular basis and are connected to your church family, because they're the ones most likely to extend invitations and essentially drive the growth of your church. We'll even discuss ways to engage people on the fringe of your community in a way that encourages them to draw people into your church.

So buckle up. I'm excited that you've decided to invest this time, effort, and energy to better yourself, to grow your leadership, which will ultimately lead to growing your church. As we embark on this journey of consistent pressure and growth in one direction and of sticking with the strategies even when things aren't going well or when you're not getting the response that you were thinking you were going to do.

Let's start by talking about something that your

church is already doing and consider how we can leverage it to reach more people in your community. We'll start the conversation considering the Big Days.

"A long time ago, in a Galilee far far away…"
THE SIGN ON "THAT CHURCH DOWN THE ROAD"

CHAPTER 2:

BIG DAYS ARE A BIG DEAL

HAVE YOU EVER noticed that the otherwise closeted Major League Baseball fans come out of the woodwork every October? Back in July, these people couldn't tell you where their local team was in the standings; some wouldn't even be able to name the leading pitcher on the team. Nevertheless, come autumn, they all step up to the plate, wearing their team's gear and cheering on the hometown team.

The same thing happens in early February when the nation's attention turns to football and speculations begin on which teams will battle it out in the Super Bowl. Again, it doesn't matter if you haven't been paying attention throughout the season—you're still going to munch on a platter of spicy chicken wings and make an unwise bet with your uncle over who's going to be named the MVP this year.[14]

By the end of February, all eyes turn to Hollywood. We tune in to The Oscars and watch the red carpet talk about who they're wearing and ultimately watch into the wee hours of the night to see who will take home that little gold statue for the best film of the year, although we haven't seen a single one (or in some cases, even heard of them).

There are moments in the broader culture when we seem to be interested in certain things collectively, and the church calendar is no different. There are days during the year when people are more likely to attend your church, and the local church leadership needs to pay more attention to those days, such as:

- **Christmas**

  It seems like people still view Christmas Eve church attendance as an annual family ritual.[15] Oftentimes, we'll see some of the highest attendance of the entire year at our Christmas services. The Christmas service is particularly important because that's when we usually have the highest percentage of unchurched people come and visit the church, so it's a critically important day on our calendar.

14 I know…I know…betting isn't good stewardship. Save your cards and letters!
15 Christianity Today & LifeWay Research say that 61% of Americans will attend church at Christmastime. In fact, nearly 80% people polled say they do it to honor Jesus! These numbers do have some regional variants, but they hold pretty steady around the country. http://bit.ly/cgf_bigday

- **Easter**

  Easter tends to be our highest recall Sunday (where people who are moderate attendees of our church will return for that Sunday service). It's an important day for us with respect to building long-term longevity in the health of the people who attend our church.

- **Mother's Day**

  Who wouldn't go to church when mom asks? This day is an important one in many churches across the country as people leverage great feelings for their moms, and as the moms try to once again help their families grow closer to Jesus.

- **"New Year" Sundays**

  There's also a certain instinct in our culture when our collective psyche seems focused on getting our lives back together and hitting new rhythms, such as Back to School or in the New Year, and these, too, become quite important 'Big Days' of the year.[16]

The reality is that—without doing anything extra—your church has several days during the year that see disproportionately high attendance.

---

16 In some churches the day that Daylight Savings ends in early November is the highest non-Holiday attendance Sunday. Even that could be a "big day" that your church could build around.

I'll confess that for the first decade or so of my ministry career, I looked down on the other churches that went all out on these days and these days alone. Somehow, I convinced myself that actually doing something special on these Big Days was somehow damaging our church's outreach. My train of thought went something like this: *if people arrived on a Big Day and saw that there was something different happening just for that day, our guests would somehow be thrown off. If we did something so different from the rest of the year it would devalue what we do on our "normal Sundays". I was fixated on the fact that "every Sunday is the best day for a guest to come to our church".* But over the time, I've come to realize the flaws in that thought process.

BIG DAYS, BIG OPPORTUNITIES

Since these Big Days represent a disproportionate opportunity to reach new people who normally don't come to your church, it's crucial that you mobilize your people in a way that ensures that they're plugged into the mission and are excited to be a part of what God's called them to. This serves as an important growth catalyst for our churches.

Generally, two things happen on Big Days:

1. **Your people are more likely to invite their friends**.

Our churches grow because people who attend our churches regularly tell their friends about their church. At the end of the day, the difference between churches that grow and churches that don't grow is that the growing churches are filled with people who tell their friends, and on these Big Days, your people are more likely to invite their friends.

2. Their friends are more likely to accept the invitation

Now, it is important to understand that 82% of all unchurched people would attend your church if they were invited to do so.[17] The sad part of this is that only 2% of the church members have invited someone to attend in this last year.[18]

If there are days during the year where your people are more likely to invite their friends, and their friends are more likely to attend, wouldn't you want to go out of your way to make sure that you maximize those opportunities?

The way we gauge the impact of an incredible Christmas service is by our January attendance. We evaluate the impact of an amazing Easter service by

---

17 I'm thankful for Thom Rainer & Lifeway Research for tracking this over the years. This stat comes from Rainer's book, "Unchurched Next Door": http://amzn.to/2gKAnlL
18 Same as the last one...great work, Thom! "Unchurched Next Door": http://amzn.to/2gKAnlL

observing what happens during the later spring attendance. How did our Back to School campaign go? We
look around the sanctuary once all the leaves are falling.

10 BIG DAY CHANNELS TO LEVERAGE

About a month before any Big Day, you need to begin
stressing to your congregation that they should be
inviting their friends. You can promote your message
across any number of channels just as long as you
keep the message intact. A simple way to accomplish
this is by writing a short blurb that contains the core
reason that your congregation's friends should attend
this particular service (or come to your particular
church).[19] You need to hammer that message repeatedly. If your church people aren't saying, "*Yes, yes, yes,
Pastor. I know. I know. Christmas Eve is going to be
important,*" then you're not simply failing to get the
message across, and you'll need to increase your messaging efforts across more channels.

(I would suggest that as you read these, that you
add at least five of these for your next Big Day that you
don't already use. The goal here is to add up to what
you are currently doing.)

1. Direct mail

I know what you're thinking, and you are right—
it is quite an old-school way to communicate, but

19 The blurb only needs to be about the length of two Tweets; that is to say, two
of the old-sized Tweets, so maybe 300 or 400 characters long.

because we are such a digital society and so much of our communication happens online, the value of personal mail has increased to quite some extent. Most of the mail that you get at home is just bad news, but what if your church put together a great direct mail piece that included a cover letter and a couple invitations designed to hand out to your friends? The letter might simply say, *"Hey, we're super excited about the upcoming Big Day. We wanted to make sure that we gave you two of these invite cards. Take one of them, put it on your fridge, and be praying for our upcoming Big Day, and take the other one, and give it to someone."* Send this out roughly four weeks before the Big Day.[20]

2. Email

Email continues to be a solid approach that can get the people moving from passivity to activity. In the three weeks leading up to a launch, you need to send at least two emails every week to your community. These emails should come from a variety of sources, so the emails that are sent out need to go under different names; they need to have different approaches so you can highlight various things leading up to the launch. Given below are a few examples of different emails that you could send out over those three weeks:

20 The thrust of this book is getting your people to invite their friends because that's really how your church grows. If you wanting to send direct mail to everyone around your church check out the USPS program "Every Door Direct Mail". It's an economical way to reach out to your community. https://eddm.usps.com

i. An email that contains an attractive graphic and the basic information about the service (date, time, etc.).

ii. An FAQ email with half a dozen questions that the people might be having about the Big Day (and answers, of course!)

iii. A message from the pastor asking for a prayer for the sermon that they're writing for the Big Day.

iv. A behind the scenes message with photos of the musicians rehearsing in order to build excitement.

v. A call to action email that would stress on how important it is to invite friends right now! (Send this just a few days before the actual service.)

vi. Send an email from the pastor the day or two beforehand requesting prayer in preparation for the service.

3. In-service time

Your announcement time for the Big Day has to be a month in advance, and you're going to require some different messages that share the same call to action for the Big Day.

I was talking to Bob Franquiz, the founding and

Senior Pastor of Calvary Fellowship in Miami, Florida after they were named one of the fastest-growing churches in the country. I asked him for the one tip that he would give to every church, and he answered, *"Be aggressive with the invite cards."*[21]

Simple invitations that have all the information about the upcoming Big Day can be placed on every seat across the entire church for the weeks leading up to a Big Day—that way, people literally have to pick these cards up before they can sit down. During the service time, you would make a quick reference to the cards: *"We've given you these invitations so you have them on hand to give to your friends."*

Another way to distribute them would be to have your ushers hand two or three invitations to everyone on their way out of the church. Make sure your ushers get them in the hands of everyone who attends!

4. Social media shareables

Generate content that drives your people into sharing it on social media. Whether it's a graphic work or a video, post it or email it and ask your congregation to please like, comment, and share on whatever social network is the most popular one at this time in your church.

Social shareables need to focus on simply getting your people to share them—not on necessarily

---

21 Check out Bob talking about what they do with Invite Cards at Calvary Fellowship here: http://bit.ly/cgf_bob

driving people with information about your services. Too many churches generate graphics or social media posts that are all about the church that just say, *"Hey, come at this time. Join this now. Come to this. Register for this class,"* and they miss the opportunity to create the content that people would want to share. Understandably, this can be quite difficult to do, but there are so many free tools online for creating great graphics (like Canva) that could create great graphic squares for you, or a design service like DesignPickle. com[22], which is an affordable service that can help you generate a bunch of graphics for you to share on various social media networks.

5. Foyer fun

People come in and out of your foyer every Sunday; you can use that space to remind them of the upcoming Big Day. It can make them slow down and think, serve as a reminder, or just be a fun speed bump on the way into the sanctuary.

For example, we did a series on Jonah called "Big Fish". In this series, we used the idea of hand-fishing for catfish in southern rivers. We bought giant 25-30 pound catfish as a way to promote the series, had people pose with them, took pictures, and shared those photos on Facebook. It got ample attention, all

---

22 Design Pickle provides low cost, flat rate design services for churches. It really is amazing…check it out.

right![23] What could you do to mix your foyer fun with social media? Don't forget distributing invitations in the foyer, too.

6. Public relations

Every December, your local media outlets are looking for stories about what the community is doing for Christmas. If you are able to craft a well-written and enticing press release *and* get it in the hands of the right assignment editor, you can generate free local press for your Big Day. In fact, most of the Big Days coincide with the few times a year that the local news sources are looking for these and such community event stories.

Public relations are often an overlooked growth channel for the churches. Of course, your message needs to look different from anything else that's happening in your community. Being remarkable, doing something that arrests their attention, and framing it in a way that will have them interested and wanting to talk to someone at your church is what's important.[24]

7. Preach on it

Before every Big Day, you should deliver at least one message from the lead pastor; this message should talk about the importance of being on a mission and

---

23 Check out the photos on Facebook today! So fun. http://bit.ly/cgf_bigfish
24 Local press is also an amazing thing to share on your social media channels. Your people will love to spread those stories online by sharing them with their friends and family. It surely makes an easy invite!

being out in the community making a difference. We need to connect the dots between why we're doing something special on a Big Day and how that connects to bringing people to Jesus. A heartwarming message one or two weeks out from the Big Day will inspire people to see that it isn't just about growing the church, but it's also about growing their relationship with Jesus[25].

Consider how you can include a commitment in this service, maybe this might look like writing cards with names of people to invite on the altar and praying for them; maybe it's texting the name of the person into the church so that our prayer teams can be in prayer for them. However, you choose to go about it, these services need to have some physical way that's moving people from just thinking about inviting to actually making a level of commitment to inviting.

8. Call people

In our pockets, we carry the world's most sophisticated communication device. How is your church using the phone to help people get connected to your church services?

A few years ago, I organized 15 people to call 2,500 of our people and asked them who they planned on inviting, if there was anything that we could do to help

---

25 Bonus Idea: Showing a video of someone who came to your church for the first time on a "Big Day" and has seen their live changed helps people imagine the impact they can have by inviting.

them (like getting them more invite cards or helping them get their friends registered for free tickets) or to do anything to really see those people get plugged in.

For a small fee, you could employ a robocall service where you can take the contact phone numbers that you have and use something like Phonevite.com and upload a voicemail, which is blasted out to all your people. However, beware that you will get some push-back from your people on this; yet, it is an effective way to get a message out.[26] Also, you can text people using a mass texting service. An example of this is Eztexting.com, which is a text blasting service where, for a few pennies per text, you can actually reach out to your people.[27]

Be clever. Think about the way you communicate and do it in a way that is intriguing, fun, and witty, and yes, please don't spam people. Use this as a channel to engage your people even if it's who you can be praying for to come to the service.

9. Engage families

The kids that attend your church have an incredible wealth of friends that they can invite to church. If the kids are coming back time and time again, it indicates

[26] An abundance of cauti: use these services sparingly. We got the best response from our robocalls when the message made fun of robocalls. We would start the message with something like "Don't you just hate these automated phone calls! But we're reaching out today through this channel because we don't want you to miss ... "

[27] The "open rates" on text messages are basically 100% still. This is a great way to reach people. But like robocalling, use it in moderation in order to ensure that your people don't get too turned off.

how much their family loves your church, to ensure that there's something special happening within your kids' ministry on the Big Days.

Big Days present the perfect opportunity to have gifts for both the guest and for the friend that invited them. Use your creativity while giving these gifts! In the past, we've had candy and prize giveaways: every kid that comes gets a bag of candy or goodies as they leave, but then they're placed in a drawing to win a giant goodie bag at the end of the service.

10. Groups and teams

Leading into the week before your Big Day, please contact every volunteer group and every community or small group throughout the church. During the huddle times, where your volunteers gather together before the service, focus on who we are inviting and how we can pray for each other as we're sending out the invites.[28] The leaders must go in first in those huddles and talk about whom they plan on inviting and how that inviting went within the small groups in the middle of the week. This is another great opportunity to pray for the community and its guests.

---

28 You are gathering with your volunteers before the service, right? We'll cover effective huddles in the Church Leadership Flywheel but they are an important part of ensuring that your volunteers feel connected to the life of the church.

SIX QUESTIONS AS YOU PREPARE FOR YOUR NEXT BIG DAY

These questions should help frame the conversations internally with your leaders as you plan for the Big Days. Taking some time with your team leading up to the next Big Day to wrestle through these questions will provide you with enough clarity on how best to leverage this day in order to make an impact on your community.

1. "How can we prepare our community spiritually?"

On these three or four Sundays, we'll have more people who our church is hoping to impact than maybe on the rest of the year, so we need to prepare for it spiritually. We need to set time aside with our core community so as to pray for these Big Days. Whether it's through the prayers, fasting, meditation, or any of the spiritual disciplines, ask the Lord to sustain you spiritually for these services.

2. "Is the message clear and compelling?"

At the core of a great Big Day experience is a clear and compelling message. It needs to be the kind of biblical message that helps the people clearly see what it means to follow Jesus in a relevant and compelling manner—this is not the day to be fuzzy or to point in many directions[29]. Practice this message portion of this service multiple times. I would highly encourage that whoever is speaking on this day gets the appropriate feedback on their message from trusted advisors who are also a proven communicators.

It is crucial that the speaker has more prep time leading into this Big Day. Ideally, there must be someone else that can speak the week beforehand, so that the person speaking on the Big Day itself has more time to prepare the message.

3. "How do we need to improve the guest welcoming experience?"

The guests can see things that you cannot. For these Big Days, in particular, we need to think vigilantly like a first-time guest. We need to look from the street all the way through to the seat to ensure that every aspect of that experience is as welcoming as possible: fix signage, paint, weed, and vacuum, as well as setting out some fresh flowers.[30]

On top of that, we also need to go out of our way with the hospitality. We must *expect* our guests, and

---

29 The sermon is central to why people attend your church. A recent study found that three out of four worshippers say sermons is the major reason that they go. http://bit.ly/cgf_sermons

30 This is where the folks at Walt Disney World excel. Have you ever wondered how, by the time you arrive at the Magic Kingdom in the morning, it already smells like popcorn right by the gate? They do that to put your brain in a "movie frame of mind"…the smell literally prepares you to receive the stories that you are about to experience. No one buys that popcorn first thing in the morning but it is put there to welcome their guests! What does the "smell" of your facility communicate to your guests?

then we must also *accept* our guests. You'd think this was a no-brainer, but sadly, it isn't. Ensure that your team is ready to accept people regardless of who they are, what they're wearing, or what isn't in their pockets. This is the day that we're opening the doors wide to welcome people in across our entire church—and truly, this should be the sort of hospitality we extend to one another every Sunday (and every day).

4. "What extra training do we need to do with our teams to ensure that it runs smoothly?"

It would be great you can have a "rehearsal" of sorts the week before; a rehearsal that would walk all of your volunteers through the worship service before-hand so that everyone feels comfortable and prepared for the Big Day. We don't want to make our people feel stressed with the idea that so many guests will be coming, but at the same time, we do need them to be hands-on about it.

5. "How can we make our kids' programming even more first-time guest-friendly?"

Unlike adult programming (where you don't need to any kind of registration), your church most likely has child registration process for parents, which it expects them to follow. Review your sign-in steps and tweak if necessary so that it is first-timer friendly—you regulars might appreciate a more simplified process, too!

Since you will be having a higher number of first-time guests, your process might need to be tweaked in order to make it run smoother with more guests than usual. Never assume that everyone who comes has been to a church before: explain everything that happens in the kids' ministry so that the kids feel welcomed throughout the entire experience.

The people responsible for what happens within the kids' ministry time also need to think through how to make it friendlier to first-time kids. I've seen churches do special gifts for guests on such days. Ensure that you have a group for first-time guests to land on, in case your church breaks your ministry into small groups.

6. "Do our guests have a firm idea of what we'd like them to attend after this Big Day?"

We need to narrow down to exactly what it is that we're asking them to come to and not have a wide variety of messages or announcements. At your Christmas Eve service, the only announcements that you should be talking about is why January is going to be the best time to come back to the church. Avoid any other messaging, and just talk about why people should come back. Hal Seed from New Song Community Church in Oceanside, California talks about how at their Christmas Eve service, all of their volunteers wear a special 'I ♥ My Church' t-shirt and tell everyone who comes to the service that if they return on the second Sunday in January, everyone who attends will also get an 'I ♥ My Church' t-shirt. (They also kicked off a new series and are doing numerous other exciting things that they talk about throughout Christmas Eve to focus their guests on coming back in the New Year— so don't worry, it's not just about the t-shirt!)[31]

FOLLOWING UP

Imagine going to an apple orchard to pick some apples on a warm September day. In fact, it's warm enough that you can feel a little bit of sweat rolling down your brow. You're out on one of those rickety ladders, trying to reach up, and picking a bunch of apples. Finally, you end up with a giant basketful, and you put them at the bottom of the tree.

You move on to the next tree and you pick another set of apples. You put those in a basket and place it at the bottom of that tree. Now, you go on to the third tree and pick even more apples. By now, you're tired and exhausted, so you take that basket to your car to bring home. You return to the second basket and you do the same thing. You drive home and realize that you've inadvertently left the very first basket at the bottom of that first tree and forgot to take it home. The difference between the apples that are at the bottom of the

---

31 It would be worth your time to check out Hal's interview at unSeminary. Wowsers! I loved what he had to say. So many good ideas! http://bit.ly/cgf_hal

tree and the apples that you took home is profound: When you get home, you store the apples somewhere cool before turning them into applesauce, apple butter, and apple pie, and within a few days, you have all kinds of new apple-y goodness ready for your family to devour.

The apples that are sitting at the bottom of the tree begin to rot in the early September heat and become a rotten mess; they turn mushy, and bees and flies hover over them.

Not following up with the people who come to your Big Day is like that first basket of apples: you've picked them off the tree, but then you've done nothing with them, and then their interest just starts to decay. The longer we take to process those contacts, the clearer it becomes that we've wasted our time with the Big Day. In the same way that climbing a tree on one of those rickety ladders to pick the apples is a waste, too, unless you take those apples home and actually do something with them.[32] It's a waste to do Big Days if we don't do something to keep a follow-up track of all those people.

We've earned the right to ask the people to return to our church; and we have, why is it the biggest mistake that most churches do when it comes to the Big Days? We celebrate when there are twice as many people at the Christmas Eve than usual, but we don't

---

32 Pro tip! Pick some apples and let them rot in a basket. Bring those apples to a meeting with your team to illustrate the importance of following up! It'll be a memorable experience! (Plus it's perfectly timed in the fall to prep your team for Christmas Eve follow up.)

try to convert that audience into January-returning audience, which means that we're missing the boat: the purpose of the Big Day is ultimately to get them connected to all the good things that are happening at your church. The follow up of the Big Days is all about building momentum, taking all of this time, effort, energy, and passion and converting it into long-term growth at your church.

INTENTION

The difference between thriving churches and churches that are barely surviving is that the thriving churches follow up with intention. They use the Big Days as an opportunity to build big momentum. Of course, getting the people to return after the Big Day needs a significant amount of time, effort, and energy for your church. What we're going to do now is talk through a simple follow up a process that everyone reading this book could easily implement in their churches.

1. Following the Big Day, make it a point to immediately send a thank you email that says, "*We are so glad you came.*" Maybe you'll include a link to the message, a downloadable MP3, or links to social media accounts where there are photos from the Big Day—just some way of sharing the experience beyond that individual day. Now, you might be wondering, "How is it

that you're going to get the emails of everyone who attends the church that day?" There are two ways you can do this. The first way: during the service, offer a first-time guest gift to anyone who fills out a visitor's contact sheet. You'd be amazed at how many people would exchange their email address for a great coffee mug or a really cool t-shirt[33]. The other way? Prior to the Big Day, ask people to register for free online tickets for events. These free tickets will give them an access to whatever service time works the best for them, but it gives you access to their email address. Even if your church is a few hundred people, offering online tickets will drive excitement about the Big Day and will help you collect the required contact information well before the event.

2. Make a follow-up phone call, or have some members of your team reach out this way. Ring them up with a simple *"Thank you so much for coming to church. We are so glad that you were a part of what happened."* Even if you are leaving a voicemail, it is okay. People will appreciate the personal outreach. Encourage people to come to the next Sunday or to whatever the next big step is.

---

33 Our church switched from giving chocolate bars to t-shirts to every "new hear guest" and we saw a 400% increase in people giving us their contact information! I guess there's something about a free t-shirt – people love it!

3. Within the next month, there needs to be a direct mailer about the next big step at your church. (Again, you've acquired their address through some kind of visitor registration.) It is particularly important to do this after Christmas because there is a wall between Christmas and the New Year where people may forget what's happening at your church, and so, a well-timed piece of direct mail by mid-January will encourage people to come back.

4. All the contacts need to land into a database system so that when the next Big Day comes on the horizon, you're out asking people to come back again. It may take people multiple years of only coming to Christmas, Easter, and Mother's Day before they finally decide to come back and stay at your church, so don't lose those contacts, nor that patience. Instead, just use the contacts to your advantage and continue extending the invitation.

Big Days are special because they only happen a few times a year. It's important that we build a strategy and system around leveraging these unique points during the calendar to see more impact in our community. We now turn to the opposite end of the spectrum and look at the regular rhythm of how we roll out the series that takes place at our church.

RAPID ACTION STEPS

1. When is the next Big Day at your church? Call a meeting this week with your team in order to talk about how you can leverage this big day.

2. Take a decision on which of the five channels you're going to add to your communications plans for the next big day. Assign them to a team member to start working on them.

3. What do you need to do for the next Big Day to ensure that your follow up was better than the last Big Day?

Středa
Wednesday

20

CHAPTER 3

USING A SERIES TO BUILD MOMENTUM

momentum
: strength or force gained by motion or by a series of events. *The wagon gained momentum as it rolled down the hill.*[34]

34 So important for leaders to think about. Merriam Webster's provided this definition: http://bit.ly/cgf_momentum

N THE FALL of 1911, two seasoned, global explorers headed for Antarctica. Roald Amundsen and Robert Scott were both at the top of their game as they raced toward the bottom of the world: the South Pole. Amundsen was attempting the conquest for the first time, whereas Scott had attempted it a few years earlier. These men underwent excellent training, staffed their teams with the most skilled people, and brought along the top-notch supplies. Amundsen was 39 years old, and Scott was 43—they were in the prime of their lives in a physical, mental, as well as an emotional sense, and were ready to take on the challenge of racing to the South Pole and returning back to tell the story. It had never been accomplished before and both these explorers were staking their legacies on being able to make this trek.

One of these teams returned home unscathed, 99 days after their departure. The other team never made it.

- Scott, a seasoned explorer, chose to push far when the weather was great. Some days, he would go as many as 60 miles under the blue skies. When the weather was poor, Scott elected to stay put, ensuring that he and his teammates had enough energy to press on when the next good day came along.

- On the other hand, Amundsen took a different strategy: he and his team would march 20 miles a day regardless of the weather conditions. He pushed his team, wore out his equipment, and used his supplies whether the skies were clear or snowy.

Which of the two strategies do you think won the race to the South Pole and made it back?

Over the years, many theories emerged pondering the difference between these team strategies. To me, one of the striking differences is that Scott's team spent a tremendous amount of time discussing what the strategy was and whether it was a good enough day to push far enough rather than actually getting down to the task of getting to the South Pole and back.

Amundsen's team knew every day that when the sun rose, their job was to march 20 miles in order get to that South Pole as quickly as they could, turn around, and come back.

In his book *Great by Choice: Uncertainty, Chaos, and Luck-Why Some Thrive Despite Them All*, author Jim Collins[35] tells the success story of the team that march focused its energy in good days and in bad days on a 20-mile march. Amundsen's team was the one that survived and returned home to tell the tale.

THE 20 MILE MARCH

The 20-mile march is an important concept that should be taken into consideration when we're trying to build momentum at our churches. We need to set our rhythms with a high enough energy output in order to make a difference towards the goals that we believe God has for us and continue to do so consistently over time to see the difference in our ministries. The trick is to pick a high enough goal that demands much from you and your team without having to face discouragement.

In the fall of 2016, Liquid Church was named one of the fastest growing churches in the country.[36] I had the honor of being on the staff at the Liquid Church for

35 Even though this book came out in 2011, it's still worth your time to process. Pick up a copy (after you're done with this book, of course!) here: http://bit.ly/cgf_southpole
36 Outreach Magazine compiles this list every fall. You can see the write up on the Liquid here: http://bit.ly/cgf_lqd

seven years and was there through our growth. What was it that God used to help us in reaching so many people so quickly? I'm convinced that our consistent focus on series promotion was a part of that equation. We gave 30 sermon series—that's nearly three years' worth of series—using the same strategies each time in order to promote every single series.

Sticking with the 20-mile march for just a moment longer, I want to encourage you to pick a robust communication approach that you are going to do every time you launch a new series and then stick with it over-time. It doesn't matter what time of year the series is happening, you need to stay focused on the same approach to promoting it. Your church grows because your people talk to their friends about the good things going on at your church. Staying focused on promoting the upcoming series in a robust manner will keep you people focused on talking about it to their friends. Don't just do this when you "feel" like it or when the timing is "perfect," but do it all year long. Do this for years and you'll see its returns in the form of new guests returning to your church! Remember, to get the job done, all you have to focus on is the 20-mile march every day.

WHAT IS A SERIES?

A series is simply a collection of some common topics that lasts for a predetermined number of weeks. Some churches have series that last just 3 or 4 weeks while other leaders are convinced on longer series lasting 10 to 12 weeks. Unlike the other ways to structure your Sunday content (lectionary, or a reading, or a simple walking through scripture verse by verse), a series approach helps your people understand where exactly you're headed next and gives them a clear picture of what's happening at your church.

There are three reasons why series preaching is an approach preferred by growing and thriving churches:

1. Google is changing the way people think[37].

Did you know that every day, one in six questions queried on Google are the ones that have never been asked before[38]? That's an amazing statistic to me, that on the day this book was written, Google received 714,697,941 new queries.[39] Such access to information is rapidly changing the way people behave, act, and think! We need to change the way that we organize our information to help people, to put it into a category, so that it can make sense, ultimately helping them to apply it in their lives. Take a moment to check out Google's "About" page[40] and you'll see a live feed

37 It's a fact! Check out this fascinating study from Harvard about how the fact that we can access basically the worlds combined knowledge in our pockets is rewiring the human brain: http://bit.ly/cgf_google
38 That's a lot of new questions...every day. Here's the reference from Google's blog: http://bit.ly/cgf_1in6
39 Want to see how many Google queries occur on the day you're reading this? Check here: : http://bit.ly/cgf_gvis
40 I double dog dare you to try to watch the "live search" feature on this page...it's hard to not get sucked in: http://bit.ly/cgf_gabout

that shows you what people are searching for. Mixed in amongst the trivia people are trying to answer are real humans looking for help with relationships, raising their kids and how to find meaning in life. These are all the questions that your church should be communicating with the people. Since people have a faster access to information, helping them comprehend information becomes an ever-increasing responsibility of the church.

2. The only thing more important than what you're watching on TV...is what else is on TV!

This was true when I was 10 years old and we had to fight over the remote. Today, it's even truer in a universe influenced by Netflix, where we're constantly bombarded with not just channels, but also hundreds of thousands of individual shows. When we lived in a 50-channel TV universe, we used to flip from channel-to-channel to try to see what else was on. The people who are coming to your church this weekend are going to wonder what's coming next: they've trained themselves to be constantly curious about what *else* the church is going to be talking about. If they don't perceive that at some point, you are going to "change topics," they will become disengaged and disinterested.

3. It helps us leverage changes in the cultural flows that happen throughout the year.

The regular rhythm of series teaching gives us the opportunity to define a regular process or system by which we can encourage the people to come. For instance, when the New Year rolls around, you'll find some people coming back to church thinking through what God has in store for them spiritually throughout the year. Preaching in series is an important way for you to structure the main content that happens at your church. It allows us to build a regular rhythm for promoting to your people and then, ultimately asking the people to come back to your church.

In a recent study, it was found that the teaching at your church is two-thirds of the reason why people attend your church.[41] Growing churches offer compelling, relevant teaching that draws people in. Teaching is vitally important to the growth of your church. Any church growth approach that doesn't have a way to leverage the core content of a church is left lacking.

CONSISTENT STRATEGIES
FOR YOUR 20-MILE MARCH

Although we mixed up the content from time to time, we applied the same core elements every month, throughout the year, which helped us develop the

---

41 Gallup did this study…it's worth chewing on: http://bit.ly/cgf_sermons

flywheel of series promotion. Below, you'll find my recommendation for what your church should do every time you launch a new series. This list has been developed through watching what worked, not only at our church but also at all the other churches across the country. As you talk consistently with your people about why they should invite their friends to this coming series, it generates enthusiasm, which is one of the goals of using a series approach. When your congregation is excited about what they're learning in the service and how they can apply it in their lives, they're more likely to invite friends and family to join in the fun. You'll see that it takes a fair amount of time, effort, and energy to promote each of these areas. It is a 20-mile march, and we're doing that because it is so critically important.

THE EIGHT ASPECTS OF A SERIES ROLLOUT PROMOTION SYSTEM

1. Give a heads-up announcement two weeks before.

As you near the end of a series that you're currently on, take some time to telegraph what's coming up next. Just like people wonder what TV show is coming up after the one they're currently watching, people will begin wondering what your church is talking about after this current series.

Be sure that when you switch from series to series, it's good to change both thematically and stylistically so that there is a dramatic difference between the two. For example, go from a relationship series where you're helping people practically to grow closer to their closest loved ones to an old testament prophet series where you're helping them wrestle through a piece of scripture that they haven't considered before. That changing of the channel helps them look forward to what's coming next and look forward to all the glorious Sundays that lie ahead.

2. Show a trailer video one week before.

One week before, it's good to play a short video trailer, which is maybe 45 seconds to 60 seconds in length, and which really asks the question that the series is going to answer[42]. What you're trying to do is set up the tension in the trailer that the series will then resolve[43]. These tools you are great not only to be used in service but also on the social media channels later. The week before the commencement of the series is critical for your people. In fact, most of the guests who will arrive at your church this weekend will make the decision within just a few days of arriving, so the bulk

---

42 Have you seen Fiverr? It's a fantastic resource for finding inexpensive videos for your church. They have a whole section of "video intro templates" where you just send the designer the info about how to you want to customize it. Check out some of these: http://bit.ly/cgf_fiverr

43 Seriously, watch movie trailers that get this right. Don't give away the punch line and don't be like a trailer with all the good parts! It's about setting the tension. Get the people to ask the question that series will attempt to answer.

of your series promotion needs to take place within right before the series starts.

3. Distribute invitations the same day you show the video trailer.

What I like to do is package these up into groups of two or three so that the people can understand implicitly that we would love them to bring a few friends to the church. Whether you place the cards on the seats in your auditorium or simply hand them out as people leave the service, ensure that each card has:

- the dates

- the times

- the locations

- a brief description of the series

4. Offer a pastoral reflection one week before the series.

It's important to slow down and articulate your pastoral point of view on why the series is so substantial. You need to show your heart and your passion for this topic and why this is an important thing for the church to be talking about. Explain why the church is headed in this new direction and take time to tell them who you're inviting—it is of critical importance that the speakers invite the people and live up to that themselves.

5. Create social shareables.

In the week leading up to the new series, really sprinkle sharable content throughout all of your social media channels. You could use your video trailer, a series of graphics, some relevant graphics—even the invitation itself! You might pose thought-provoking questions related to the topical series. The big idea here is *to stir conversation*.

6. Have team huddles

The week before you roll out the new series, take some time to slow down and gather your team and committee leaders to find out who they're inviting and why they're excited about the upcoming series. Take time in those huddles to pray for the speaker as well as the listeners.

7. Direct email—three days before the service

Since you've done so much promotion over the past few weeks, this email is really just a quick reminder to invite friends before the series can be launched. The reality is that most people who will visit your church will make the decision to come in those days; they're not planning it weeks in advance. This is why it becomes so crucial that we inform multiple times, leading up to these last three days, and then we ask them to extend the invitation right before the weekend (for instance, on a Thursday).

8. The "Saturday Before" email

We did a study at unSeminary that looked at 81 churches and asked, *do occasional emails sent to churches the Saturday before a series launch, does it help drive attendance?*[44] We found that it does. This tool of sending an email on Saturday, around noon, the day before the series is launched can be a great way to remind the people to do last minute asking. In the Saturday message, recall and echo the speaker's passionate message from Sunday morning. There are many ways in which you can approach this; two simple ways including a request for prayer or sharing a behind-the-scenes photo of the pre-launch.

PLANNING FOR VARIETY
IN THE MARCH

Stay consistent in your promotion strategies, but incorporate variety into your sermon series. What we don't want to do is get caught in a rut where we're talking about the same thing repeatedly; so the question that stands is, how do we achieve variety within a theme? How do you plan a set of series for variety? Here are four ideas that you need to keep in mind:

1. Survey your people.

What does your church want to learn? How do they want to grow? Learning what they want is the first

---

44 You can check out the results and the snappy infographic here: http://bit.ly/cgf_saturday

step, and figuring out what they truly need is the next—and it's an incredibly significant puzzle piece. Often, attractive churches receive the following criticism: they are just trying to tickle people's ears or only talk about things that the people are interested in. The reality is that = many people find sermons offering practical life applications to be more engaging. Practically speaking, you can do this in any fashion that makes sense for your people (e.g. SurveyMonkey, program insert, social media, et cetera). In time, as you shepherd your people, you'll get a sense of where the people are and incorporate those issues and subjects into your sermon series.

2. Check out the best-seller list.

When you're trying to figure out what it is that the people are thinking about, just take a quick peek at the non-fiction best-sellers lists in The New York Times, The Washington Post, or The Wall Street Journal. These lists will reveal a host of issues and topics burdening the masses, which you can use to inspire a sermon series. Look at what's selling on Amazon and start seeing that website as an idea search engine of sorts, instead of treating it like an online marketplace.

3. Consider the whole counsel of God.

Can we just be honest for a moment? I know that as preachers, we all have certain topics that we get excited about or prefer talking about—and our congregations sense this, too, because we tend to give messages on those topics time and time again. Maybe we feel comfortable talking more about the Old Testament prophets than we do talking about Revelation. Perhaps it's easier for us to delve into Paul's epistles than it is for us to broach the Sermon on the Mount. As you plan your series, plan to push yourself to a place that is outside of your "usual." The preachers, too, need to grow and develop their individual spiritual lives.

That doesn't mean that you necessarily need to take the message that's the most exciting for you and file it away for the next three years. On the contrary, keep your coming back to cornerstone messages that you want to the world to hear—but don't make it the weekly blue plate special. Find a way to weave that into the highest times of the year where people begin thinking about inviting their friends.

The series that resonate the most are the ones where the teacher is the most excited about the content. If you're disengaged, your people will most certainly be disengaged.

4. Add one-offs in between series.
There are messages that your church ought to hear regularly (or at least annually): tithing, stewardship, evangelism, service. There are also calendar dates that fall into this one-off arena as well, like the Mother's

Day, or even Thanksgiving. Many denominations have special services for things like All Saints Sunday or the Transfiguration, so these are built-ins. These important topics and special days in the life of the church don't disappear just because you're trying a series approach; likewise, you also don't have to shoehorn these into a particular series. Actually, having these one-off or two-part specials can be a great way to add variety to your schedule, an act that will only draw in more people.

A WORD ABOUT WORKING AHEAD.

One of the lead pastors that I worked with, and who will remain nameless for this story, used to plan only about a week ahead on his messages. Early on in our time together, we were slated to start a brand new series on a Sunday morning. We had new programs printed, new graphics to support the series for our video screens, and the band was even ready with music that complemented the series launch. I still remember coming that morning to find out that our pastor wanted to add just one more week to the end of the previous series! We made some quick changes and that morning, our community was a bit surprised that we had just one last message of the series when we had already told them that we were moving forward onto something new. Obviously, it was not exactly ideal, but we rolled with it.

We lost a little momentum on that change, but it taught me a lesson that I've carried with me for a long time: there is a tension between planning ahead and responding to what the Spirit wants to do in the life of a local church. From my seat, I would always love for our church to be 2-3 months ahead on what series we were planning to do next. Being that far out gives us lots of time to maximize our promotional efforts so as to ensure we deliver an excited audience ready to receive the messages. However, most teaching pastors want to reserve the right to respond to how the messages are landing in the community. They want to remain fluid and be able to see how they can develop their content in harmony with the needs of the people that they serve. This is a tension to be managed rather than a problem to be solved.[45] We should be aiming to grow the advanced planning we're doing as a church but realize that all plans should be held loosely.

Obviously, the further ahead we work on what series are coming up next gives us more time to apply creativity to this aspect of the church growth flywheel. If you've been to any church leadership conferences where this comes up, you'll hear the leaders talk about the fact that they are planning 6-12 months in advance. When you drill into that more closely, you'll often hear that they really know where things

---

45 Watch this video by Andy Stanley: The Upside of Tension http://bit.ly/cgf_tension

are going 3-4 months from now and that they have great levels of clarity on where the next 6-8 weeks are headed. You need to work towards this level of planning in your church. Once you get to this level, the pressure needs to be pushed towards working further in advance. Over time, you'll settle into a place where you are able to work ahead enough to maximize the effort being put in and still allow enough flexibility for the teaching to remain responsive.

RAPID ACTION STEPS

1. What could your "20-mile march" in the series promotion be? Spend an hour nailing down what you're going to do and then start working on the next series!

2. Planning ahead makes series promotion more effective. What would it take to double how far in advance your messages are planned? (And then double it again a year from now!)

3. Start observing closely to some of the fastest growing churches in the country. What are they doing regularly to promote their series that you could incorporate into your strategy?

CHAPTER 4:

SOCIAL IS FIRE, CONTENT IS GAS

"When I hear people debate the "return on investment" of social media? It makes me remember why so many business fail. Most businesses are not playing the marathon. They're playing the sprint. They're not worried about lifetime value and retention. They're worried about short-term goals."

- GARY VAYNERCHUK

I N JUST TEN short years, social media changed our society forever. And in the process, it also changed the church growth profoundly. When I first started in ministry over twenty years ago, it was literally inconceivable to fathom the impact of a digital social network. During those days, just a few of us were involved in supposedly geeky things like the email; today, a church that doesn't have a social media strategy is just lagging behind. My friend and colleague Peter Gowesky from Hope City Church in Sarasota, Florida, is a brand new church planter, and it has been fascinating to watch how social media has been integral to his entire launch strategy from the ground up. I've been reminded as I've watched him use Facebook to connect his people and reach new groups of people why social media is critically important regardless of the size of your ministry!

As we look into the future, there's no doubt about it: we need to integrate social media as a core part of the church's growth strategy.

A BRIEF HISTORY

As I sit down to write this chapter, I'm a bit overwhelmed with the task before me because social media is a constantly evolving platform. Back in the early nineties, I remember connecting to FidoNet with my 300-baud modem through a local BBS, where we would send messages to each other. There was a magical feeling about exchanging written messages with someone else living somewhere else just over a phone line. A few years later, we all became members of CompuServe, an early online service provider that gave people the opportunity to do a wide variety of activities into live chat, trivia games, bulletin boards and so much more! In 1996, an Israeli firm launched ICQ[46], the first widespread chat service that allowed you to make instant connections from your desktop with people all over the world. LiveJournal, launched as one of the first blogging platforms, was groundbreaking in its idea, for the concept of writing a diary online for the entire world to read was a radically

---

46 Who else still has that sound stuck in their head? Uh-Oh! Listen in for old time sake: http://bit.ly/cgf_uhoh

new notion. Just a few years later, the world came to know Friends Journal, the first significant modern social network that paved the way for the social networks of today. In 2003, Myspace swept the Internet. I chuckle a little thinking about a good friend of mine spending hours grooming his band's page, talking to the fans, leaving comments, and interacting in a way that encouraged people to connect with their band. Myspace showed us how social networking took place on a large scale.[47]

The very next year, Facebook launched out of Mark Zuckerberg's Harvard dorm room[48]. I still remember being at an event with students where they were talking about this new service called Facebook where they could instantaneously gather both online and in the real world. In 2005, YouTube introduced the idea that anyone could upload videos for other people to see, integrating a clever social underpinning where people were encouraged to comment on posts and to share each other's videos.

Somewhere around 2007 or 2008, it was as if the social web had exploded. Facebook continued to dominate and grew by hundreds of millions of users, and then a wide variety of social networks tried to work their ways into our lives, seemingly overnight. In

---

47 Looking for a fun conversation about the history of social networks? Check out this article: http://bit.ly/2BurtBr
48 Keep an eye on this. Starting with the youth market is critical for social networks.

2010, Instagram launched an app without a social layer but then became a full-blown, photo-driven social network. Immediately after, in walks Twitch, the first to-do live streaming at scale and encourages people to watch each other play video games. Imagine that, people sitting watching other people play video games. It really is an amazing world we live in, and a whole variety of other networks—Periscope, Meerkat, Marco Polo.

Why is he giving me this history lesson? I know this stuff, I remember this stuff. I was around.

There's an important distinction that I want you to understand about social networks: people are social and want to connect with each other, and all of these online services are getting better at helping people become social and make the right connections.

It's important that we aren't sold out to one network because these networks will come and go. Whether it was my friend and his band spending time on Myspace fifteen years ago, the Instagram gurus who were socially acclaimed for curating excellent feeds last year, or the SnapChat stars doing the same thing today, people jump from network to network both online *and* in churches. Change and grow with your community as the people you are trying to serve change and grow, but always remember that at the end of the day, we offer people a chance to connect with the message of Jesus and the timeless community of Christ.

As I step back and look at how all of these networks have developed over the years, I see their common traits—these are traits that we can apply if we take into consideration the impact they can have on the growth of our church.

GENERATING ENGAGEMENT

I just took some time to look at my Facebook feed and I was amazed at what I saw:

- A post from Julia, a friend from a small group from about ten years ago. Julia and her husband are friends, but I see them more in the online world than I do in real life.

- My friend Greg, a church consultant who helps people craft their front-end guest experiences, was asking people for feedback on a project that he was working on.

- My wife Christine posted a series of cute pictures of our children from seven years ago when they were so little.

- Some guy named Jason was talking about something that happened with a football player named Zack Miller.[49]

---

49 I'm not sure at all who this Jason guy is…or how he ended up in my feed!

- Hillsong posted about the Hillsong team box subscription service that they were selling.

So, why was this amazing? This is just a typical review of a typical Facebook feed, right? Maybe, but it's still amazing to me that a short scroll through my feed is more than just a stroll down the memory lane: it's really the touch point for all of my worlds colliding on one screen! Talk about connection—social media plugs in parts of our lives, even the parts that we have to be reminded of (like the mysterious Jason).

Now, stop and think for a moment what that means for your church and for my church. Our content needs to intersperse between the closest relationships we have, it needs to fit within the relationships that people have for our work environment, and to reach our fringe relationships. How can a church generate content that will arrest people's attention? It's important that you have the right mindset in your approach to social media in order to use it correctly to leverage growth.

With the exception of LinkedIn, most of the social networks start as youth movements. Many have over one hundred million users, which really is the critical mass that you need to take into consideration. If a network hasn't reached 100 million users, it's not really worth considering. The value of social networks is in its ability to connect with the people. The more the people connect, the more valuable it is. One hundred million active users mean that you probably know someone on it. This is a phenomenon known as network effects (which basically means that the more people that are on these networks, the more value they have). You want to be looking for networks that have a high level of adoption in the communities that you are attempting to reach. Don't be weighed down by what the church down the street is doing, but look instead at which networks are making their way into the schedules of the people that you're trying to reach.

Look at where your people are. For instance, maybe there's some obscure network that not many people are using, but for some reason, this is the network that has blown up in your own community. As you hear from your people, you may see certain trends that you ultimately to want to be a part of that.

After determining which social networks resonate with your people, the most important question that comes is: what kind of content do we need to put on to the social media? See, in a very real way, these social networks are blazing fires, and one of the church's job is fitting in between various friends that are on these networks by offering great content that accelerates the social sharing that happens on these networks.

Social networks are fire while the content you produce is gas. The goal is to spread the content on social networks; content that your people will pass to their friends and will see their friends connected with.

We have two options when it comes to the types of "spreadable," or in other words, there are really only two kinds of gas that we can pour on the social media fire to help it spread. The first is remarkable (the kind of content that is such creative, stunning magic that people want to share it) and the second is helpful (the kind of content that ultimately, people want to share because it solves the real world problems).

REMARKABLE CONTENT

One of the best examples of remarkable content that I've seen in a long time comes directly from the commercial marketplace: the Oreo dunk-in-the-dark image from the 2013 Super Bowl. You might remember it, too. If you're not a huge football fan or if a lot has happened in your world since 2013, here's the recap: during the 2013 Super Bowl, there was a technical malfunction and the lights went out. Well, the Oreo marketing team went into overtime and generated a simple graphic that looked like the lights had gone out with the simple words that read, "You can still dunk in the dark." That one image was retweeted hundreds of thousands of times, and it's been estimated that there were tens of millions of dollars gained in advertising gained because of the sheer number of times that this graphic was shared (and because of people like me who subsequently talked about it repeatedly). This small piece of social media was truly remarkable because it did two things: it captured the moment (and not just any moment but the one where a hundred million people were watching) and it entertained people enough to make them want to share that entertaining moment with others[50].

Remarkable content is amazing when you can do it, but **it is difficult to generate because you need to have the magic combination of creativity and timing.** This is a great and lofty goal for most churches to attain, and you might have already figured that while it can be difficult to generate, it is necessary that we strive for it on a regular basis.

At Liquid Church, we tried multiple things over the years that we were hoping would be remarkable enough that our friends would want to share. One Christmas, we did a Star Wars-themed Christmas Eve service. I know, I know, some of you might be already checking out saying *"What does Star Wars have to do with Christmas Eve?"* Well, we planned this cosmic as a fun for families as we celebrated not only the release of Star Wars in the broader culture but also asked people to focus on to the cosmic story that was being told on Christmas Eve[51]. Leading up to

---

50 Another way to think about this campaign is that Oreo did a superb job getting people to talk about it after it happened. In fact, the "after game" conversations about this social media content had generated much more value for them than the initial retweets during the game. People like me talking about propel the myth…I'm doing it again. How meta! Here's a video from the Wall Street Journal talking about it too: http://bit.ly/cgf_dunk

51 Before you write this off as told "attractive church heresy" make sure to watch Pastor Tim's message on Revelation 12. It's so sold…and so fun! http://bit.ly/cgf_cosmic

that night, we were playing all kinds of fun graphics and videos on our social media channels in order to capture people's attention. We set up a video team to serve up a number of funny Stormtrooper videos, where we had Stormtrooper costumes and also had Stormtroopers sort of botching various Christmas situations: Stormtroopers burning Christmas cookies; and Stormtroopers doing a terrible job decorating the tree. These were fun videos and it was remarkably funny to watch the combination of Stormtroopers in what looked like a normal suburban family life, trying to get ready for Christmas time[52]. We knew our people were trying to get ready for Christmas time, and we know that sometimes we feel like bumbling idiots trying to get things ready at our houses. The video team did an incredible job with the production, and the people loved it. They hit the mark on remarkability, and they encouraged people to attend our Christmas Eve service. They really accomplished what we wanted to accomplish.

Another church that produces remarkable social media graphics on a regular basis is The Cause Church from Kansas City, Missouri. This church regularly generates stunningly beautiful photography and overlay graphics that are second to none. They are engaging

---

52 Comic writers tip: All comedy is either normal people in strange situations or strange people in normal situations. Basically, all of Saturday Night Live is built on these two premises. In these videos, we had Stormtroopers in normal domestic situations…so funny!

because these graphics show not only the images of the church engaged in what the church does but also beautiful scenes and scripture from the messages that the pastors give on a regular basis. The simple beauty of these designs is enough for people to want to post and share them with everyone.

Elevation Church—particularly Pastor Steven Furtick's Instagram feed—really is off the hook. They've set the pace with a great combination of visually appealing designs playing to Pastor Stevens' arresting communication style. Clicking like, commenting and sharing is very easy with his videos because they're visually stunning and quite easy to understand.

The problem with creating remarkable social media is that it's not scalable—it's unpredictable. It's very difficult to generate award-winning, high-quality social media consistently. The church growth flywheel is about giving you things that you can do on a regular basis, things that all of us churches can do, in order to push forward and reach out to more people.

HELPFUL CONTENT

I would rather you focus your time and energy on doing things that can actually benefit the people in your community. This content is the sort of thing that answers questions or helps people with the real-world problems. The good news about this is that the church often finds itself in the position of a helper in our communities. We are naturally wired to want to reach out and to solve problems and answer people's questions.

River Fiberglass Pools is a great marketplace example of this. They tell the fascinating story of Marcus Sheridan, who was faced with a great economic down-turn in 2008 while selling fiberglass pools (a luxury product). He turned to the Internet and decided that what he would do is start answering questions about his product, and in the process become the place to go to when anyone needed answers to their questions about fiberglass pools. In just period of two years, the business' website went from the standard twenty-five pages to publishing over eight hundred articles on the social media, all loaded with information about fiber-glass pools and backyard paradises. Around the same time, the organization went from spending $200,000 on advertising down to $20,000, but went from two million dollars in sales to 4.5 million dollars in sales—*and this was all during the great recession*. The thing that Marcus Sheridan found was that by simply being helpful, he was able to reach people on the social web in a way that is more predictable and more scalable than just simply trying to be remarkable[53].

There are a plethora of churches that are doing a great job by providing helpful content. One of my favor-ites is The Meeting House in Toronto, Canada, a church

---

53 Want to watch a bit more of this story? http://bit.ly/cgf_pools

that I was privileged to be a part of for years as we were launching out multiple campuses. In the recent years, they've launched an online content initiative called 'Bruxy's Bag of Questions,' which is a series of online videos answering questions that people may generally have[54]. The last time I checked, they had close to ninety videos and close to 90,000 views. These videos are all somewhere between 4-8 minutes long and tackle just one question each; the questions are generally like, *is there a difference between demons and fallen angels? Why is the Bible filled with so much polygamy? Why did God allow Adam and Eve to sin? Why do Christians believe God has to be three in one? How can we love our enemies without being a doormat? Why do Christians love to fight about the details? Should Christians avoid violent media? Why does Jesus get away with being angry? Are Christian pacifists just playing it safe? Are some books of the Old Testament still relevant?*

I love that this kind of video content plays to Bruxy's strength, which is answering questions. At the end of every message on every Sunday, he has offered an open forum Q&A for about 30 years now. These videos are really taking that strength and repackaging them up for a social media-friendly delivery.

Follow The Meeting House on Facebook or on YouTube and you'll see people sharing these questions with their friends regularly. It is a near-bottomless pit

---

54 You really need to go and watch some of these: http://bit.ly/cgf_bbq

of resources because people will always have more questions, and there are always new answers to give!

NewSpring Church in South Carolina also provides incredible content. For years, NewSpring has been generating articles or blog posts that are inherently designed to elicit conversations with people and to push a new content angle regularly. For instance, they address important and relevant topics like how to look forward to the future even at mid-life, or three practical ways to remove comparison from your life, or how to fight for a contentment while you're single, or the dangerous way in which comparison can make you prideful, or why it's important to stop running from silence, or Jesus runs to the mass. On a regular basis— multiple times a week, even— NewSpring publishes blog posts like this. As you can see through their various channels and even on the blog itself, people are sharing this kind of content, and they are doing it frequently. Bringing helpful content to the forefront of your social media usage is a long-term way to build up your social media presence. Over the time, not only has this content proven to be great on the social media, but it also is fantastic for Google because they are seen as an authoritative voice—Google is where people go searching for content and looking for their answers.

WELL, WHAT ABOUT YOUR CHURCH?

What is some practical content that you could be generating on a regular basis?

What kind of content could you make to help your people connect with you online while also helping them connect with their friends?

Let's not forget that the church grows because people tell their friends. We all know that at its core, the reason why people come to our church is that their friends invite them. Social media is a fantastic opportunity to tap into for church growth because your people are already there, and they're talking to their friends! What we need to do is generate content for your church that can get your people talking.

Examples to try:

1. Share behind-the-scenes content.

You'll be amazed at the response that you'd get when you share photos of your team preparing for a weekend or praying before the morning service. It doesn't matter what social network you choose to post these photos on; for some reason, this quick peek behind the scenes is incredibly sticky for people because they will be witnessing something that they normally don't. A great time to use it is, especially, when any of the Big Days is approaching. If you're coming up on a Big Day, showing the church doing physical preparations around the church is the kind of thing that your people would love to share and love to see.

2. Repurpose the existing content that you have.

I am almost hesitant to include this here because the topic itself is so much bigger than a few simple paragraphs.[55] One of the things that have struck me over the years is how the churches generate a tremendous amount of content every weekend but do very little to repurpose it and use it again. What you *should* be doing is finding ways to reuse that content! The message, the verses, the sentiments—you're already using them, and it's likely that you can use them again, so consider how you can "update" that content in newer, and fresher ways. You should be generating quote squares with a simple tool like Canva. Often times, the messages will have sticky statements in them. Well crafted statements that bring the entire message down to a few words. This is a great kind of content for you to repurpose during the week.

If your church audio records the message, you need to ensure that those messages find their way on the social networks. If you have a video recording, do the same thing—post it! Your church could use Facebook and the Facebook Live tool to simply retell certain

---

55 I could probably write an entire book on how your church should be repurposing the content that it makes. Hmm…thinking…thinking. (Gotta finish this one first!)

pieces of the message throughout the week, which will literally spread from you to your listeners and then it could be as easily spread to their friends.

3. The Q&A Format.

I strongly suggest ripping off The Meeting House and this question-and-answer format, and trust me, they won't mind, they're good people[56]. Take their format and apply it in a way that makes sense to you. You could email it to people in your church and ask them *what are the three questions on your mind that you wish us to answer*? Then, simply take all those questions and start working through them. You may not have the resources to produce videos like The Meeting House, but that's okay—you could address these issues and provide the answers in written and posted blog posts. Maybe you generate a new question each Monday, and every week brings a new answer comes out. The key to success here is to really provide questions and answers that are relevant and practical for your community and keeping them confined to a format that's helpful, brief, as well as digestible. If you're not much of a writer, you could shoot a video using something like a Facebook video or even just your iPhone. Take that out, record your answer, and upload it online.

---

56 They really are amazing, if you ever get a chance to visit them it would be a great church for you to visit on some weekend.

4. 'What to expect content.'

If people haven't been to your church already, they'll often wonder *what am I going to expect when I arrive this weekend*? They're not sure. It's not clear to them what it's like to come to your church. The 'What to expect content' is simply shareable content that your people could pass along to their friends. It could cover topics like:

- What to expect when you arrive at our kid's area?

- What to expect at your first communion service?

- What to expect for our upcoming Christmas Eve?

- What to expect when you arrive at our parking lot?

Think of the various aspects of your church and just generate content that revolves around answering 'what to expect?' Again, these could be written blogs, a photo series, or a quick video. This type of content is highly sticky. It's the kind of thing that people like sharing and it's a great resource for your first-time guests, too.

YOU NEED TO BE SOCIAL

You need to interact with people – plain and simple. As we discussed earlier, all of these networks are just platforms for people to connect with other people. Each church must do three things when they are trying to figure out the social side of the social networks.

1. Respond to every comment.

Nearly every social network offers some way for people to like, comment, and share content. You have to go out of your way to ensure that someone is responding to the people. Ultimately, people *will* feel better about your online presence as you interact with them, and the more frequently you interact with your followers, the better your rankings will get on all these social networks. As the network sees that you're following people and interacting with them, they will ultimately want to push that ranking up so that people see your content more often.

2. Share other people's content.

Don't be greedy. Don't just share what's happening at your church; share what's going on around in the town. If there's something great happening at the local farmers' market, it will be fantastic if your church chooses to share that, or if there's another church that's doing something new, ensure you share their content and point people not just to yourself, but also to others. If there are authors who have written books that you enjoy, it would be a wonderful thing to share on your church's social profiles.

3. The 3x3x3.

Here's a strategy that I like to use: what you do three days a week is a direct message (DM) three of your followers and ask them if there is any way you could be helping them. Is there a way you can pray for them? Reach out to your people on the direct message function of the social network and ask them if there's anything you can do. The next step is writing something on the public profile of three of your followers. Don't just write anything, post up something that you appreciate about them. This is a great thing to do with your volunteers. Every week, log on to the church profile and write on three people's profiles (people who volunteer for the church), telling them that you are thankful for their time, for their willingness to volunteer, and so forth. If you do this thrice a week, guess what? You are instantly becoming more social in your social network, and it will continue to draw more and more folks.[57]

---

57 What I really should have said was to just follow my friend, Kenny Jahng, on any social network and just do what he does. He is the Jedi Master of social interaction. He helps people at scale. It's breathtaking to watch. Study what he does and just repeat it: http://bit.ly/cgf_kenny

MY RECOMMENDATION

However, I really do think that you need to start with what networks your people are on and build it up from there. Beyond that, there is one social network that every church should take into consideration, and that network is Facebook. Did you know that two billion people are active on Facebook every single day?[58] That's a staggering figure. Just take a step back and think about what that means. *Two billion people.* Over 50% of adults in our country use Facebook on a regular basis. 40% of women browse Facebook on their phones before even getting out of bed every morning. This network has a massive influence on many different demographics.

One of the most amazing statistics about Facebook is everyone on Facebook –all two billion of those people – is only 3.4 connections away from everyone else[59]. It's no longer the six degrees of separation. It's the new, 3.4 degrees of separation. This is a powerful thing for us as we try to grow our churches. Even if your Facebook page has just a hundred followers on it, there literally are thousands and thousands of people within one or two links from your followers or group members. Don't be discouraged by the number of people that are following you—instead, remember

---

58 We talked earlier about this stat...look back for the reference! ;) Check out this cool live counter of Facebook users: http://bit.ly/cgf_fbnumber
59 Wowsers. That really is amazing. http://bit.ly/cgf_3half

that all of your followers have friends whom you can reach out to.

This is about getting your people to connect with their friends and generating content that your people will ultimately want to share. If your church isn't on Facebook right now, getting a Facebook account for the church would be the best thing for you to get started. Now, if your church is on Facebook and you're not posting at least daily, if not multiple times a day, increase the frequency of your posts. The reality of it is that all of these networks are hungry for content.

As we wrap this chapter up, I want you to stop shying away from social media. You might have gone all this way through and you're still resistant to the idea of your church spending more time, effort, energy, and maybe even money on its Facebook account or other social media presences. Stop shying away from that. What would you do if there was an event in your town where 60% of the town's population was attending enthusiastically? Would you want to be there? Of course, you would. You'd show up just to see what's happening. Well, the reality of it is, 60% of the people in your community are on social media every single day[60]. It doesn't matter how big or small your church is right now, and it doesn't matter where you're located—this is the truth of the matter. **You're missing an opportunity if you don't embrace this as a**

---

60 34.6% of statistics are made up. ;)

massive mission field for your church. Remember, help is much better than hype. You need to think of yourself as a content producer that's generating helpful content on a regular basis that your people ultimately want to share with each other.

In the next chapter, we're going to move away from digital for a while and look at a very practical, hands-on kind of way that your church can engage with its community. In fact, we're going to move you from thinking about social justice and community engagement as a pure way to reach out to people in your community as well as a vitally important aspect of the church growth flywheel. Your church needs to reach into your community to see people getting connected with your church. Let's look and understand how we can just be the cause.

RAPID ACTION STEPS

1. What would have to change in your church in order to look at social media as a mission field rather than a "nice to have" promotional channel?

2. Which of the engagement strategies we talked about in this chapter could you put into place this week at your church?

3. All of our leadership teams have "that guy" or "that girl" who "isn't on Facebook". Get them to read this chapter and then take them out for coffee to see what you can do to change their mind.

CHAPTER 5

BE CAUSE

"Preach the Gospel at all times.
When necessary, use words."
ST. FRANCIS OF ASSISI.

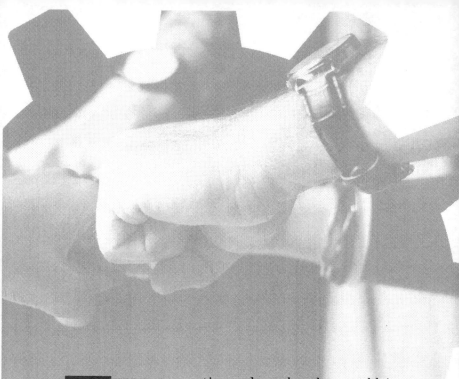

THERE WAS A time when churches could just open their doors and the people would flood in. Most folks were churchgoers, and they often attended whichever parish of their chosen denomination was closest to their homes. You'd see families walking to the church in sidewalk communities; you'd see the parking lots fill up in the morning. The church played an active role in the neighborhood it served: it wasn't a social club; it was the center of the community service and it offered ministry and sanctuary to those who needed it the most.

Why does it feel like those days are long gone?

Have you ever stopped and wondered what is it that will work today to put the church back in a leadership role within the community? How, in an ever-increasing secularized context, can a church reach out to the largely secular community of today?

There was a time when you could picture the faith makeup of your community like a rectangular table. At one end of the table were the Christians; the other end was maybe the Jewish community and down the sides were all the other faith communities. Really, the Judeo-Christian mindset was really seen as a broad way to understand faith in our community life. However, this model no longer applies. Instead of a rectangle, the faith community now resembles a circle where the Christians and our Jewish brothers and the other multiplicity of faiths including the rise of the nones has come to the point where the church no longer holds a place of prominence within the community[61].

By all measures, the voice of the church is dwindling. We need to look that fact squarely in the eye if we want our churches to make an impact. We can't ignore the fact that people aren't coming to us anymore[62]. When was the last time that you heard a church leader named to a list of community leaders or movers-and-shakers within a town or a city? It's sadly comical that so many places see their local high school football coach as a leader; most of the areas hold these guys in higher esteem than any pastor. Still, I refuse to

---

61 Even just writing this seems laughable. We've come a long way since being at the "head of the table"!
62 Check out the beginning of this book for a reference. 94% of all churches in our country are losing ground against the growth of the communities they serve.

be down, feel humdrum, or think negatively about the church. I really do believe that the local church is the hope of the world[63]. When the local church does well and then continues along that path, it becomes a truly unstoppable force for the good in our communities.

Why do I want to see your church restored to a place of prominence in your community? Because I believe that Jesus' message is transformational and ultimately, it is the only thing that will make a difference in the lives of our people and in the places that we serve.

We've been trying to study closely the patterns that we see in growing churches that have made an impact, such as the communication and marketing initiatives that the churches are growing used to on a consistent basis. Over time, you begin seeing patterns that emerge across the wide variety of growing churches. The question I want you to ask is this: *how do those patterns apply to your church*?

Our churches grow because of one simple reason: people tell their friends.

It really isn't any more mysterious than that.

CHURCHES THAT AREN'T GROWING VERSUS PREVAILING CHURCHES.

What's the difference between the dying churches and prevailing churches? The latter is simply more remarkable. I mean that in a literal sense, as in

---

63 Hat tip to Bill Hybels for this repeated reminder!

thriving churches are literally *worthy of the remarks of the people who attend them.* Those churches have things happening that people tell their friends whether they're in the schoolyard dropping off their kids in the morning or sitting around at the barbershop on a Saturday morning or watching the little league game from the bleachers. Growing churches are worthy of remarks, and over time, your church must become more remark-worthy. You need to find more ways to have your people talking to their friends about what's happening at your church.

If you were to study some of the fastest growing churches in the country over the last ten years, you will notice a subtle undercurrent that explains why these churches are growing. Not only is this an undercurrent, a brilliant tactic, but it also honors God and communicates wisely with the people that are around us. I want to challenge everyone who's reading this book to apply this **concept to his or her** church.

Frequently, you'll see the Elevation Church in Charlotte, North Carolina listed as one the Top 10 Fastest Growing Churches in the country[64]. A Sunday morning visit would offer possible explanations into why the church is growing at such an exponential rate:

- Pastor Steven Furtick is a **charismatic and engaging communicator.**

---

[64] You should be tracking along with these churches: http://bit.ly/cgf_outreach

- The **worship music is attractive and highly energetic.**

- Their services **are built with tons of anticipation**.

- Their kids' **programming is the best**.

- Their **student ministry is among some of the most innovative ones** in the country.

In many ways, the Elevation Church is firing on all cylinders when it comes to being remarkable.

Since its inception, the Elevation Church hosts what they like to call the Love Week. It's a weeklong outreach event held in late July or early August, and the church partners with over two hundred organizations to host about as much as a hundred events. Year after year, the Love Week invests millions of dollars in community service hours in partner organizations as the church challenges the people to get out of their seats and into the streets. Over the years, Elevation has received incredible press coverage as the local media continues to notice that this church isn't just getting people to attend its services, but it's also moving them out to make a difference in their communities. It's become such a hallmark event that people travel from all over the country to North Carolina every summer in order to help this church reach out to its community.

There are three lessons on community engagement that I draw out of Elevation Church's Love Week:

1. Partner with local organizations.

Rather than trying to develop from-the-ground-up ministries or social service agencies, a part of the genius of Love Week is that it seems to be fueling people, money, and resources into the existing organizations. The church sees itself as an empowering conductor of the amazing things happening in the community rather than looking to draw all the attention to itself. It sees itself as a helper to the community[65].

2. Service opportunities are highly visible.

Every person that participates in the Love Week receives a snappy t-shirt. The events are the kind of thing that you want to take pictures of with your friends. They're the kind of service opportunities that look great on video. Who doesn't want to be seen rebuilding a homeless shelter or repainting a playground across the town? In fact, every year, you can see that the Elevation Church invests a considerable amount of time with its photography and video teams in covering what's happening and spreading the news – not only for that week but also for the rest of the year. The other churches can learn from this: we want to make serving our community so attractive that the

---

65 This is a part of why I believe God honors Love Week at Elevation Church. Rather than wanting to see it all about them, they ultimately are trying to help other organizations.

people in our church will want to be a part of it; we want to make it the kind of thing that will spread from something internal to something external.

3. Everyone is encouraged to be a part of Love Week.

Because of the wide variety of service opportunities, last year, close to a hundred events, spanning across different times of the day and at different levels of complexity, were held. Everyone who's a part of Elevation Church is encouraged to serve in at least one event. (Of course, many people volunteer more often than that depending on their work schedules and availability). Each event sets out to be fun, to be the kind of thing that the people will want to spend their time doing. Elevation Church is attempting to make their community service as exciting and engaging as their weekend services.

I want to challenge your church to think if there is anything like the Love Week that you can do. How can you drive more community engagement to get your people to serve on a regular basis?

GOD THINGS = GOOD THINGS

I want to tell you about the proudest day in my entire ministry career so far. On October 29, 2012, Superstorm Sandy rolled through the Tri-State area. As a church leader in New Jersey, I was well aware of the fact that this storm had affected not only the people from our church but our entire community. You could feel the collective tension across our entire state and in Pennsylvania as well as in New York because of what had happened here. I still remember sitting at a diner one morning with our leadership team after the storm. We had all just dealt with our own homes and our own issues, but we sat there looking at each other and there was this deep feeling in the air that was strongly suggesting that *we need to do something*. As a church, we felt called for to reach our entire region with the gospel of Jesus, and we were convinced that we needed to step up and find a way to help.

Out of that early meeting came a Sandy Thanksgiving. It was a rather simple idea – we asked people to use their Thanksgiving Day to help people who had lost everything. The results were amazing. Over 1,500 people from our church woke up on the Thanksgiving Day and went to Staten Island to serve families that had suffered losses from the 20-foot waves that blew through their communities. We cleaned out people's homes, helping them take all of their worldly possessions out to break down their buildings (the buildings needed to be broken down back to the studs in order to begin the rebuilding process).

You can trust me when I say that it was utterly excruciating to watch people's physical and tangible memories being put into giant dumpsters, picked up by front-end excavators, and thrown away. We knew it wasn't going to be pretty that way. Knowing that, we also hosted street parties throughout the entire Staten Island; these parties were full of barbecue meals, music, balloons, tables decorated with table-cloths and accoutrements. You'd be amazed at how communities came together around small little par-ties that we threw in the middle of a disaster zone. We felt Jesus, and we hoped that they did too. Here He was, His church going into some of the darkest days of these people's lives to throw a party. It felt like a great honor to watch the communities come together. At the end of those parties, we left everything—the supplies and the barbecues, all of it—for the people who were still on those streets[66].

We spread the love of Jesus, and we didn't do it through preaching, but through our acts of love that reached out.

Now, our church was able to participate in such an amazing day because we had been involved in mass mobilization for many years. During our free market, we asked our people to come and bring their best stuff to give away (instead of selling). We collaborated with the local social service agencies and actually gave those donated items away to people who lived on the margins of life. On a similar note, we also sponsored

---

[66] It was an amazing. It was surreal living through this and while it was hap-pening I was telling myself "this is probably going to be one of the best days of my life!" Wild.

a 5K where all of the proceeds raised money for the people who did not have an access to clean drinking water on the other side of the world. Not only did we raise tens of thousands of dollars, but we also heightened the public awareness of a critical issue. Once, four hundred men from our church showed up to fix up a battered women's shelter. In just twenty-four hours, our men tried to show these women that they could put their strength to use for something good as they undertook the task of completing an extreme home makeover. I also recall another time of service where our preschoolers worked alongside the senior citizens and everyone in between to pack a quarter of a million meals for the community food shelter. At the end of those events, we threw big parties where we invited the entire community to celebrate what we had accomplished together[67].

We realized that we could take what we had done in the past and apply it to what was happening here in after the Superstorm Sandy. On Sandy Thanksgiving, we ended up getting featured on CNN. Every hour on the hour, they came to us to cover various aspects of what was happening. We generated interest in our church as people discussed online about the church that had come out to help in this community.

See, our communities view these services and events as good things. We see it as a God thing, but what we

---

67 When Jesus is involved, it always seems like there's a party close by.

want to do is find a common ground, a place where we can connect with the people in our community.

The reality is that the only way to make an impact in an increasingly secularized world is being Jesus on the move. As a church, make a collective impact to mobilize people in mass service events to make a difference together. It's this sort of difference-making that grabs people's attention. Certainly, it's sad that the church isn't known for making a difference like this anymore, but your church *should* be and it's the kind of thing that will ultimately draw people to the church.

FASTEST GROWING CHURCHES ARE DOING IT.

There's a consistent pattern that can be observed with even a cursory look at the fastest-growing churches in the country, and that pattern suggests that mass mobilization efforts **(this is an idea of mobilizing a large percentage of its adults to make an actual impact in community initiatives within their community and abroad)** are a regular part of what happens at those churches.

- **The Crossroad Church in Cincinnati** hosts a large-scale Thanksgiving Food Drive. Just last year, they brought in enough food for over 60,000 Thanksgiving dinners. They've also taken on the church-wide responsibility of sponsoring over 6,000 children in a developing country. This church has been declared to be the fastest-growing church in America for two years in a row by Outreach Magazine, which shouldn't come as a surprise when you see a church doing so many good things in the community.

- **The Eastside Church in Anaheim, California,** is one of the fastest growing churches in the country and has even won that title for multiple years in a row. Compassion is listed at the top priority and concern on this church's website. It's right up there with messages and giving. In fact, this church has done so much community outreach that a documentary called Bravely Forward is now being put together to tell the story of all the various things that this church has accomplished.

- **Red Rocks Church in Littleton, Colorado** runs an event called Hope for the Holidays, which is essentially a gift drive and wrapping event. The church and the community wrap up and deliver thousands of gifts every year to various social service agencies in the community. The church also runs a prison ministry known as God Behind Bar in which, the men of the church bring the hope of Jesus to the prisoners.

- **The Traders Point Church in Indianapolis, Indiana** runs a special needs prom where they annually help young adults who could never go to a prom to experience one. This particular prom requires three to four volunteers for every guest that comes; it literally requires more volunteers than the number of guests in order to run smoothly. That night, you get an opportunity to see the last become the first.

- **The Next Level Church has locations all across New England**, in a part of a world where frankly, the church just doesn't exactly grow. This church is exploding and launching new campuses all the time. They did a gas buy-down event where they offer gas for 80% of the normal price at a time when the price of gas was so high. Their lead pastor, Josh Gagnon, said, *"God said it's better to give than it is to receive,"* and they realized how important something like gas can be, so when the price was high, the church mobilized its people and its financial resources to make a difference in such a practical way.

Are you still unconvinced that your church must think about some mass outreach opportunity? There are usually two groups of people that I run into that hesitate to take this on:

- The *"Aren't we just supposed to preach the gospel?"* group. To this group of people, I'd ask them to think about what their church does to make a difference in their respective communities? What means are you employing to attract people to your church? I presume that if you're reading a book on church growth, your church has done a number of things in an attempt to make itself and its messages accessible to the people around you. You may have modern music or maybe you even have fancy lights. I remember going to Willow Creek Community Church in Chicago during the 1990s, and at that point, Willow was doing a lot of plays and skits as a part of its teaching. The idea was to try asking questions and engaging people in a different way than the churches had done before. At the very base, community engagement is like that music that you play on Sunday morning, those fancy lights, and even those nineties-era skits. Even if, for some reason, you're scared of social justice, put it in the category of great music or fancy lights.

Remember that Star Wars Christmas Eve I wrote about earlier? Now, a part of that story that I didn't tell you earlier is that for two weeks prior to that, we did a community outreach service where we packaged up meals for the poor in our community. We had close to two thousand people come and serve the community that day, but what's even greater is that we actually had more first-time guests come to the meal-packing event than we had at our fancy Star Wars Christmas Eve.

- The *"Isn't this inefficient impact?"* group. This group doesn't need convincing that to social justice is an important thing; on the contrary, these people know that the opposite of poverty is justice. They know that we need to serve people relationally and it gets the heebie-jeebies when you talk about putting toys in small shoeboxes and shipping them to the other side of the world because, in their opinion, *all you're doing is exporting commercialism.* This group looks at this kind of community outreach suspiciously because it engages such a large percentage of people. In fact, it feels inauthentic to them because it doesn't smell of the people that it's trying to serve.

To these brothers and sisters, I want to say, *"Listen, we want to move more people into an active life of compassion. I do understand that there are people among us who have spent their lives serving the poor, but our churches are filled with lots of people who don't have any part of their life oriented towards serving others, and what we need to do is to create the kind of experiences that we move people step-by-step towards a life of compassion."* At often times, our community impact friends want to just push people from the shallow end of the pool into the deep end right away— or maybe worse, into the raging ocean—and they don't understand that adults need to be often be eased into this kind of lifestyle change.

WHERE TO START?

1. Find three or four logical times of year to schedule your events.

These events are such a large-scale impact on the church that they simply cannot be done well more than three or four times a year. Look at the Elevation Church, which is a church of nearly 30,000 people. They conduct the Love Week once a year because they know they need to do it in a high-impact time. What you want to do is team up the times of year when people are looking for opportunities with the times that make sense for your church.

Any time of the year can work, truly. Christmas seems to be the time of year when almost all the people are thinking about serving. During the spring, people are looking to get outside and to try something different and new. Summer works well too because people are looking for things to do with their families. What you need to do is pick three or four times of year that you will take a run at this.

2. Meet with public officials.

Start by reaching out to a public official in your community. This could be a mayor or even a school board superintendent—try to meet with the highest level of a public official that you can, and simply ask them how your church can help. At Liquid Church, we did this at all of our campuses as we tried to develop opportunities over the years, and I could tell you plenty of true stories of how various community officials were just blown away by the fact that a church would come to them and ask how they could help (usually, people come to the mayor wanting help, not wanting *to* help). It's disarming, encouraging, and exciting for a public official to help guide a church towards what they can do to help the community.

3. Collaborate with other organizations.

As I've partnered with many organizations over the years, I've never once experienced any of the organizations refusing hundreds of volunteers and tens of thousands of dollars to fund their projects. Look at this as an opportunity to give back to those partner organizations and to serve not only three or four times a year with this high-impact, highly visible, fun outreach events, but also follow-up with regular relational, smaller, more personal, more one-on-one service opportunities.

4. Get all hands on deck.

These events are all consuming for your church. This isn't a job of just one committee, and ideally, it shouldn't even be. This isn't for just one part of the church or one team. Everyone needs to lean in, from the senior pastor right down to the youngest of the kids. You're going to need to assign a project manager – someone who will wake up every morning and think about how they can make this event better. The goal here is to get as many of your people involved as possible. Make sure that you design your events such that families and people of all ages can join in and help.

5. Rinse and repeat.

Well, how do we leverage this sort of service opportunity for growth? How does this help our church be remarkable? How do we set this up to ensure that it will help the people connect to your church? If your event takes place in the spirit of "just getting people to come to your church," it won't really work. Start with one and you'll be amazed at how infectious it becomes. Just be the cause. Get the people to move from their seats into the streets and your people will start talking about it.

TIPS FOR HOSTING A
REMARKABLE EVENT

Getting out into the community has positive ripple effects not only for your local church but also for The Church. As believers, we need to work together in order to turn the impression of the church around from being stodgy, disconnected, homophobic, anti-caring, and insular to one vibrant, connected, loving, and engaged in the community. How can you turn a large event into something that is beyond large, that is remarkable?

Get tee'd.

I know it sounds pedantic and almost low level from a strategic point of view, but teams have uniforms and what you're trying to do is call every member of your church to a team; so give them a t-shirt. This also ensures that when your people are out serving, they're recognizable as a group. This also spreads well when you're taking pictures for the follow-up later.

Capture the event for sharing on social media.

This needs to be an assigned role where someone who's great with a smartphone takes pictures and videos, shares them instantaneously, and then also curates those images for sharing later. You also need to have an eye for capturing stories throughout this event. Look for ways that your church is making a difference. Look for people in your community that are reaching out to say thank you and capture those stories so that ultimately, you can turn around and celebrate with your people.

Celebrate.

You cannot over-celebrate this. Make sure that the event itself takes place in a spirit of celebration. Don't just serve the community but ensure that your people have a good time while doing it. Make sure your leaders are thanking people incessantly; that you're so honored that they've given time to come and to be a part of this event. Then take time in your Sunday services that next week and for weeks, possibly months later, to celebrate the amazing things that your church has done. Talk about it when you do the annual reviews. It really is amazing what your church has done and you want to celebrate it. You just cannot over-celebrate it.

Preach it.

As you're leading into the event, make sure that you're mobilizing your people using the core message on your weekend services. Then sprinkle the stories that you've captured throughout as illustrations of what your church has accomplished in the community.

The Evangel Church in Scotch Plains, New Jersey, has an event every fall known as Service for Service, where they cancel the Sunday morning church services and to have a Sunday morning church of service. For weeks leading up to that Sunday, they canvas their neighbors and ask them a simple question: *"How can we serve you? What is a way that we can reach out to make a difference?"* On that Sunday, the church members go out to paint fences and clean out garages and cut grass and rake the leaves. The church takes this service and turns it into an act of service.

I'm inspired by churches like the Evangel Church that understand the difference that community engagement makes, not only in the lives of the community that it serves but in their own church community as well, as we move people from a life of inward, insular, self-focused to ultimately focusing on other people. Really, ultimately, the question to be asked is, how do we get the right message to the right people at the right time?

RAPID ACTION STEPS

1. Can't jump into the deep end right away? Why not contact one of the churches that I've talked about in this chapter and take a group from your church to serve with them at their next mass mobilization event?

2. Why are you hesitant to do this? Are you really willing to do anything to reach people with the message of Jesus? Why are you resisting getting your people engaged in this way?

3. Don't start small. Think about a big need in your community and figure out how to mobilize the most of people towards it. Your church is too important to think small.

CHAPTER 6

THE RIGHT PEOPLE GET THE RIGHT MESSAGE AT THE RIGHT TIME.

"The single biggest problem in communication is the illusion that it has taken place."
GEORGE BERNARD SHAW

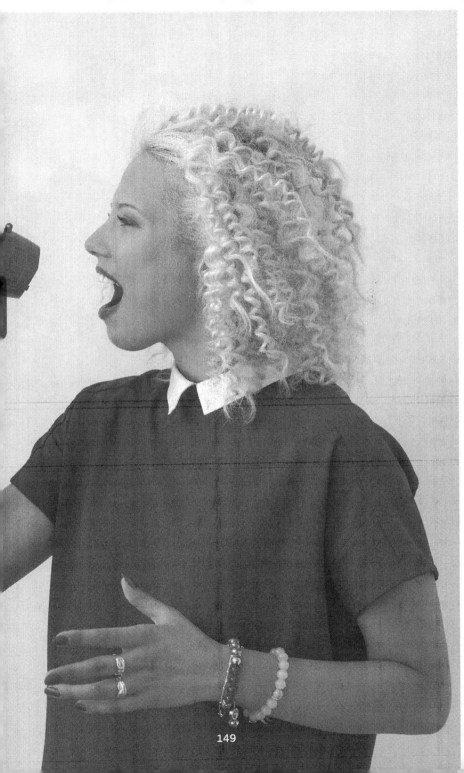

I'S IMPORTANT TO have a discussion of how the church talks to itself. You see, we've talked about this earlier in the book, about how our churches grow because our people talk to their friends about coming to the church.

At the end of the day, that's really all of it. It isn't any more complex than that[68].

At their core, the churches that grow, prevail and make a difference in their community are simply the churches that their people want to talk to their friends about. Most of this book has been about ensuring that your church is doing remarkable things and ensuring that you're getting the right information to people. Now it's time to hone in on the specifics of where

68 Classic…It took me 30,000 words to get to clarity.

the church growth connects with church health and church leadership. You see, as we think about the growth of our churches, we need to figure out how can we plug people in and connect with the church.

Most church leaders think about the front door when considering how our churches grow. We think the front door—these are the visitors who come for Big Days or who come just for a special series. Of course, we want to do whatever we can to make that front door as wide as possible.

But what about the back door?

Growing churches are obsessed not only with the front door but also with the back door. How do we get people to stick with us and stay? How do we get them to become a part of our church community? Although I won't be getting into a full-fledged discussion in this book on how to close the back door at your church, I do want to provide you with some ground rules for understanding what growing churches do to help people **stick and stay.**

COMPELLING STICKINESS

All the growing organizations contain three types of people, and these are the three groups that you must develop within your church:

1. Raving returners.

These people come back to your church repeatedly. These are the people who show up four out of four Sundays; they're even there on that fifth Sunday. They come to worship in the middle of the summer. While you're thinking to yourself, *"If it wasn't for being paid today, I think I might be at the beach,"* Raving Returners are the kind of people who can't get enough of your church.

Growing, prevailing churches have plenty of Raving Returners. They have the kind of people who are willing to come to whatever the church does and are always excited to be a part of it. A part of what we want to do as church leaders are to cultivate the Raving Returners because they are the people who commit to being a part of everything at the church.

2. Sneezers

Like a second-grader with a bad cold that keeps sneezing and spreads it among everybody in their classroom, the Sneezers are the kind of people who just can't help but spread the virus of the church. When a Sneezer is in the queue at the grocery store, they will chitchat with the cashier (and all of the other people behind them in the queue as well), and they're quite effusive in their discussion about what's happening at your church. Sneezers love to talk to people in other clubs, boards, or organizations in the town about the great things that are happening at your church. Sneezers are viral, and they share quite regularly. They may not always show up to your activities, but they *are* constantly sharing everything that is happening at your church. They even go out of their way to try to see other people connected to your church.

Sneezers are vital because they do a disproportionate amount of the inviting at your church. In fact, identifying those Sneezers at your church and ensuring that they share the church news regularly is important! We know that only two percent of all people in our churches share on a regular basis, and it, therefore, becomes imperative to find those two percent who attend your church because we want to give them the right information at the right time so that they'll tell their friends all about it[69].

3. Advocates.

Now, these people aren't necessarily the Raving Returners, but they *are* the kind of people who support and love the church. They think it's a great thing to be a part of it and they're happy with what the church is doing. At the same time, the Advocates are strategic thinkers who go out of their ways to advocate for the church in the broader community. These people might even be political leaders in the local town (or perceive themselves to be an equivalent mover or shaker).

69 LifeWay has done great research on how people talk about their churches. Here's some more of it: http://bit.ly/cgf_two

They're the kind of people who analyze the situations and develop ways to have the mayor to show up to our outreach at the end of the month. The Advocates are concerned with how the church is utilizing the local paper, the Facebook page, and the radio station in order to invite more people to the church.

Although they may not attend the church every Sunday or come to all the special events themselves, the Advocates are important to find because they're going to invest their time and intellectual talents in helping people understand and connect with what's happening at the church on a regular basis. The Advocates can be powerful in your local town, as they advertise and promote the good things that are happening at your church.

Raving Returners, Sneezers, and Advocates represent about ten percent of your total church. This is a radical minority, but this ten percent includes the people who ultimately tell others about your church. In the same way that it doesn't take half of the country to elect a president, it only takes about a tenth of your church body to really help you push your message forward.

It is important to realize that although you're engaging the entire church, it's an "all-skate." In other words, all of these activities are trying to get everyone to engage, share, and talk about the church. While we're at it, we also need to focus on the radical minority who are really going to carry this message the farthest through the conversations. This ten percent—a.k.a., your radical minority— is the people who are the fervent core of regular church promotion within your local community.

As we're thinking about communication and church growth, it's very easy to start dwelling on the people who are filling your sanctuaries and auditoriums every Sunday. Your mind might jump to the roster of small group leaders, Sunday school teachers, and musicians since these are the faces that you directly interact with regularly on a one-to-one basis. Instead, consider the smaller portion that really is doing a different kind of heavy lifting. They might not be in leadership positions within the church, but they are truly the leaders when it comes to talking to the community about your church.

5 POWERFUL STEPS TO
CLOSING THE BACK DOOR

Anyone who has the experience of running a website will tell you that they focus their time, energy, and money on trying to attract visitors to their website and compelling them to stick around, and sign up for email updates, or buy a product. Oftentimes, they'll even throw in a freebie (*10% off with your first order! Download this ebook when you register!)*

Although this really isn't just classically a church growth strategy or a front door strategy, it really is the beginning of trying to shut the back door. It's important for us to take it into consideration here. Now, I'm not going to be able to deal with an entire new-here process in this book. However, I do want to give you a few rules of thumb that your church must implement for this area of your church.

New-here process. An important piece of the church growth flywheel is ensuring that when your invitees arrive at your church, you are set up. This will make them feel both accepted, and expected. I'm talking about this in this book, because it really doesn't make sense to attract guests to your church, and then not do anything to receive them when they arrive. I've been to just too many churches where they're working hard on the front door in that they're doing all kinds of crazy things to get the people in on a Sunday morning, but then they're not doing anything at all to try to get those people plugged into their church.

Your church needs to average as many first-time guests through an entire year, as you have on average on any given Sunday.

Here's the equation:
new visitors per year = # of people from an average Sunday morning

In other words, if your regular church attendance averages two hundred people, you should expect two hundred guests throughout the year or about four new guests each week. Likewise, if you typically have a thousand people show up for the Sunday services, you should see a thousand guests throughout the entire year. (You can do the math and figure out what that looks like for your church.) If you are not seeing that many documented first-time guests at your church, then you're frankly not doing enough front-door activity. You need more new guests.

Of course, this begs the question, *"How can we tell the number of guests that are coming?"* because the truth is that while some guests will be more than happy to raise their hands or fill out a guest card to drop in the offering plate, the majority of guests would rather sit back and observe before they hand out their contact information. It's common for the guests to slide in and not necessarily make themselves known. Well, there is an industry standard implemented across many churches, approaches, denominations, and backgrounds that has proven itself the most effective way to help guests to identify when they arrive: the gifts.

1. Gifts

Let's just be honest: people getting something for *free*, especially when they see the gift as something of value. If you're not already doing so, offer your new-here guests a gift as a reward for filling out a guest information card. Do this is during the service, at every service, every

Sunday, all year long. Ask whoever makes the announcements to direct everyone's attention to the information card. Maybe it's in the seat in front of you, maybe you distributed one to everyone who came in; perhaps it's in the bulletin. Wherever it is, that "new-here" card is a way that can connect you with your guests. Simply invite your guests to fill out their information and take it out into the foyer where they can exchange it for a guest gift. Give them clear instructions on where the gift is, and also let them know what the gift is.

Now, let me say a few words about the gifts: they're important. At Liquid Church, there was a point when we saw about two thousand people on a Sunday, but we were giving away around eight hundred gift bags every year. We were giving away chocolate bars along with a small bag of information about our church. We started looking at the contents of the bag and considered how we could improve them. Since these gifts help register more guest information, we actually switched from giving away chocolate bars to giving away T-Shirts. The following year we went from 800 to 3,500 new-here guest information cards. What an incredible jump! Obviously, the budget committee members were a bit concerned because the difference in cost between a chocolate bar and a T-Shirt is high, but we thought it was worth it since we gained better information about our guests as they arrived.

Now that you have a way to contact your new guests, what are you going to do?

2. Follow up

Build a simple follow-up process so that you can connect with these guests on a regular basis in the upcoming days, weeks, and months in order to encourage them to come back. The people who visit your church won't automatically think that they should come again. In fact, some people will come one time and that checks a box for them in their world, and they won't be back. Connect with them as quickly as possible—as soon as Sunday afternoon isn't too early. When we launch new churches or a new campus, I always recommend that the campus pastor tries to connect with the new visitors that Sunday night. The pastor could send a personal email, make a direct phone call; he or she could even wait until Monday or Tuesday if you feel that very Sunday night seems a bit too aggressive. Whatever way and whichever time, acknowledge the gift of their attendance. If people have gone out of their way to give you their contact information, it means they're raising their hands and saying, "It would be great if you'd connect with me." This is not the time to be shy or hesitant.

3. Ask them back

Make sure that you directly ask them to return. Extend this invitation by phone or email or send a card (just make sure it arrives at the end of that week). A big part of closing the back door involves breaking the cycle of non-attendance. People are not used to attending your church, and you'd like them to get used to it and start attending regularly. The second-time visitors are an incredible gift to your church. In fact, if you can get someone to attend a second time, the likelihood that he or she is going to make your church his or her church home increases dramatically. On the third visit, there is a glorious spike in this possibility.

4. Create a database

You want to make sure that you manage their information in a database over an extended period so that you can loop back around and re-invite those people to come to your church for new events and the Big Days. There will be people who will only attend on Christmas and Easter—*and that's really okay*. What we want to do is make sure we're inviting them throughout the entire year so that they can realize how we're going out of our way to let them know they're always welcome. Of course, you and I know they're always welcome, but sometimes it helps if the guests are reminded of it.

NEW-HERE GUESTS VS. FIRST-TIME GUESTS

You'll notice throughout this conversation that I've been talking about the new-here guests, as opposed to the first time guest. I'm a big believer in the language of the new-here guest because it allows people to opt in when they say that they're new here, as opposed to being there for the first time. If your entire process revolves around people identifying the first time, you must know that some people just won't identify themselves. However, if you said *new-here*, it might be someone's second or third visit, which means they're still "new here." Maybe they came once at Easter two years ago, and now they've come back because they actually want to check it out. Perhaps they visited last month but never filled out an info card and are more willing to give you their contact info now. Whatever the case, the *new-here* encompasses a broader spectrum of visitors and thus reaches more of them.

A system for getting people into teams, and groups.

Once your church crosses the threshold of 200 people, you need to work diligently to ensure that the people are developing relationships with each other. There have been volumes written on the importance of small groups, and the importance of serving in a local church for helping people stay connected to that church. Suffice it to say, having people serve at your church and plugging them into a small group is a critically important aspect for the visitors to make the jump from occasionally attending your church as opposed to making the church their chosen place of worship. Growing churches commonly communicate with the new-here guests about serving on a team or joining a particular group.

We are seeing the emergence of an industry standard in this area. There are a number of variants on this, but we're seeing people come out of their new-here process and plugging into opportunities in order to learn about the church and to make friends with other people who are attending the church. Sometimes these are billed as 'new member classes' or Our Church 101, but what is covered in these classes can vary from church-to-church. The goal is to try making these experiences paint a clearer and more vivid picture of your church. Some of the topics might include:

- What is it like to attend your church?

- The vision and values of the church.

- Why is it important to get onto a team or into a group?

- The best way for them to get the most out of this experience.

Some large churches run these courses every Sunday, while the other smaller ones offer them once a month. There is something about providing classes regularly that helps people connect. If you only do a new-here class once a quarter, and someone can't make it that night, they're going to go almost six months before they can have that specific opportunity to know more about your church. That's just far too long. Doing them monthly seems to be able to balance the difference between doing them so much that your team can become overwhelmed, and do them so little that you end up not providing enough opportunity to the people to plug in.

The other advantage of doing them monthly is that you'll have a smaller group to work with, regardless of the size of your church. Leading a smaller group meet gives the leader an opportunity to get to know the people in this class, which happens to be the overall goal anyway – building relationships.

Let's consider again that your church has 300 people coming each Sunday and you average 300 new-here guests a year. To break it down, you'd see five new guests on every Sunday. If you offered an orientation once a month, that would give you the opportunity to have about 20 people in your classes.

Now let's say you get half of those people to show up to your class every month; that's 10 people. The rate of people connecting to a team or a group is very high coming out of one of these monthly classes, 70 or 80%. Clearly, this can be an important part of how you assimilate the new-here guests into members.

A conversation about church announcements.
I am a church announcements fanatic. I love that part of the service. Over the years, I've had opportunities to coach with many different churches, and I'll usually, on a Sunday morning, go get a chance to "secret shop" their experience. The announcement portion of the Sunday morning is the part I love digging into because then, I can actually help the churches improve.

Most churches have three major portions of their Sunday morning experiences:

1. Music and worship, which helps people transcend and connect to the divine.

2. Teaching and the message, which helps people transform and understand where God has been and where He wants to take them.

3. Announcements, which is all about moving the people to action.

The announcements part of Sunday morning is capable of moving people out of their seats and into the streets of the church. It moves them from having an internal relationship to making a heartfelt, whole-life connection to the Church. The announcements shouldn't be a secondary, small part of the service. In fact, they are just as important as the music or the teaching. There is nothing holier than people taking action on their faith.

There are five pieces of announcement advice that I give to the churches regularly[70]:

1. Narrow the focus.

You're probably talking about too many things on a Sunday morning. Most churches would, outside of the teaching, have some sort of offering call. They'll also want to do some sort of new-here announcement, where we acknowledge the guests. They also might have a prayer portion of the service that talks about the people in the church that are in need. Then someone usually gets up and rattles off three or four, or heaven forbid, maybe six or even ten different items about what's going on in the life of your church.

Stop it.

This is a bad idea.

Time and again, studies have shown that the more options we give to the people, the less likely they are to pick any of them.

So what should you do instead? Only mention one thing.

(I know that sounds crazy.)

Take the time to connect with hearts, and ensure that people understand why, whatever you are announcing, is so important to them.

---

70 We've talked a lot about announcements over at unSeminary...drop by there for more help: http://bit.ly/cgf_announce

2. Engagement.

This part of the service should always be about getting people to engage in the life of the church. This is not a time to give updates on what's happening. The punchline of the announcements should always be *here is the next step you need to take in your church.* Don't talk about the weather. Don't talk about the sports game from last night. Be on the task.

Make eye contact, use humor, have a truly engaging conversation about the one calendar item you're discussing in your spoken announcements. We wouldn't want a worship leader to lead the musical portion of the morning, and not care if the people in the audience are engaging with the music. The same is true with the announcements portion: if people aren't moving to action, it only means that our leaders aren't doing their job. The output of every announcement needs to be to fill out a card, check out a box, text a page, some sort of call, text, a link. It has to be some sort of call to action that moves people to connect with the life of the church.

3. What's in it for me?

Can we get real for a minute? I know this may rub you the wrong way, and in fact, there are people that probably might put down this book just because of this reason.

All humans are selfish. You're selfish, and I'm selfish.

In fact, our internal wiring leans towards *what will make life better for me*. That's humanity.

Now, in the life of the church, we want to move our people beyond that. We want people to live a selfless life. We want them to live a life focused on other...but that's not where people start when they come to our church. They start selfishly.

Our job must be leading them from there and taking them to a life of selflessness. In our announcements, we need to be clear what's in it for the people we're addressing. If we're talking about the upcoming youth group event, don't just say, "We've got a youth group event coming up." Explain why you're doing the youth group event. Let the parents know that you're hoping that the young people in the life of your church will gain new friends and that going to this event will help your students make the kinds of friends that the parents in your church would love to have.

Every announcement needs to be wrapped up in a healthy dose of why. Why is it important to the people who are listening? If you can't clearly articulate and you make an emotional connection to what's in it for the audience, simply don't do the announcement.

- We do small groups as a church so that you can foster deeper relationships.

- We host Bible studies so that you can understand the Word in a clearer and more concise manner.

- We have volunteer opportunities in our kids' ministry because you're going to love helping other kids connect with the teachings of Jesus.

Start and end every announcement with what's in it for our audience.

4. Slow down, and clarify action steps.

Take it from somebody who has spent hours watching the church people make announcements over the years.

We've warmed people up, we've connected with them, we've engaged them, and we've told them what's in it for them. We've made a logical connection; they understand why they should plug-in with whatever the call to action that we're doing... then we roll over how it is that they're supposed to connect. We aren't clear with them about the actual steps that we need them to take.

This is a botched opportunity. We've invested all this time, effort, and energy to help our people feel connected, and then we miss it in the execution when we are at the last mile. You can't make it too clear or too obvious what you need people to do. If you are asking your new-here guest to connect in the foyer, make that place in the foyer as obvious as you possibly can. Signs are fantastic. Show people what the sign looks like, point to where it is, go out of your way to make it straightforward. Put up a tent or a banner that has *new here* written on it in giant letters. If you're asking people to sign up in order to serve in the kids ministry, hand out a postcard to everyone in your church, and let it contain just a very simple form with a picture of kids on it that says *I would like information on serving in kids ministry.*

Strive to reduce all the friction of sign-ups on your website and in your physical environments. A friend of mine worked for a major courier on the design and development of online forums—that was his team's job. They've seen all the mistakes made over the years and have worked hard to make those forums as simple as possible. He once said something that has stuck with me ever since, "You can't underestimate how humans over-complicate things. So dumb it down, make it simple. Slow down."

Churches mess this step up because they're usually just talking too quickly, trying to communicate too much information in too little time. Slow down, and communicate in a way that makes it obvious for the people what they have to do next.

5. Be remarkable.

Whoever is doing the announcements needs to think about how he or she can do this in a way that will get the people's attention, and tell their friends about. *How can we give the announcements in a way that will drive home the point in a creative and engaging manner? How can I be remarkable?*

A simple way to do that is having clear and comparing visuals every time you get up and do an announcement. Props are an amazing way to drive home a clear message. Bringing guests up on the stage to help you with the announcements is another great way to be remarkable. The human brain is a pattern recognition machine. Our job, as communicators, is to be close enough to the pattern that people aren't thrown off, but then to do something different than they are anticipating.

If you're talking about an upcoming movie night in the church for elementary kids, why not walk in with a bag of popcorn? The unmistakable aroma of popcorn will grab their attention. Rather than just having a picture of popcorn, have actual popcorn on the stage. (Bonus points: you could actually pass some out to people in the first few rows or ask people to raise their hands if they're going to be coming to the event, and hand them bags of popcorn right in the middle of the service.)

The last part of the communication puzzle that keeps the right messages in front of people at the right time. What does your internal communication look like? How can you improve this part of your church?

RAPID ACTION STEPS

1. Do the math. How many "new here guests" is your church seeing? Is it higher than your average attendance?

2. What aspect of this chapter can you put into action right away this year?

3. Announcements! What do you need to change this weekend to better leverage this aspect of your service to move people to action?

CHAPTER 7:

NOW WHAT?

Sam: "This is it."
Frodo: "This is what?"
Sam: "If take one more step,
it'll be the farthest away
from home I've ever been."

WAS SITTING ACROSS the table from a church leader[71]; this guy is the kind of church leader that I love: he has read a bunch of books, been to a bunch of conferences, and he was really trying to see his church make a difference, to break through. **You see, this church leader had seen their church grow for a number of years but then, had started seeing a plateau.** In fact, the church was starting to stare down a slight decline.

I asked about their numbers. *Tell me about the size of your church and the number of guests that used to come on a regular basis. And tell me about what your 'new-here' process looks like.* I asked what they

71 No footnotes in this chapter…because basically this whole chapter is a footnote to the book. Have you enjoyed this footnote conversation throughout the book? I'd love to hear from you! Email me: rb@unseminary.com

were doing to attract people to the big days. *Talk to me about how you're advertising the upcoming series.* Over the next hour and a half, we wrote all over the tablecloth. Well, actually, it was craft paper, and we were writing with crayons. (I love fancy restaurants like that.)

We talked about the conversion ratios, regular processes, how to use Facebook, the role of video, billboards, and a whole bunch of other tactics and strategies. As we drew to the end of our time, the church leader leaned back and looked at all the stuff that I had scribbled all over the craft paper, and simply looked at me and asked: "Now what?"

It was at that moment that I realized that I needed to write this book.

You see, we tend over-complicate how to go about growing our churches. In fact, what I realized over that lunchtime was that I had made it sound way more complex than it actually was. I overloaded and over-burdened this leader with a lot of different tactics and strategies. I talked around in circles about the various things that could be considered and really probed a bunch of different ideas. What I realized was we needed to develop a system by which the people could repeat to help see their churches grow.

As this church leader sat across from me at our crayon-covered table with a bewildered look on his face, I realized that perhaps I had done more damage than good. Instead of helping, I had hurt because I wasn't being clear on what steps they should take towards seeing their church grow.

Friends, your church can grow. The Church Growth Flywheel is all about providing you with a repeatable system that you can do that you can put into place now.

As we said at the beginning of the book, this is a thousand-day process. You're not going to grow overnight. It's going to take you a long time to get all of these aspects of the Church Growth Flywheel working in harmony. But if you were to invest this coming year in saying, "We're going to improve each one of these five areas. We're going to invest to make all of these areas work," imagine the difference that you could bring about at your church. Imagine what would happen as you begin gaining the momentum.

My hope is for you is to come to the end of this book, and actually lean back and say, "That's it? It seems so simple. It seems so straightforward." Yes, there are many steps, but it's not complex. I really do believe that that's the truth.

I shared an insight earlier that can make all the difference in your church, an idea within that if applied could make the difference in the life of your church. You see, I don't think ideas are that important; I think taking the ideas in this book and actually applying them is what's important.

What will really make the biggest difference is when you and your team get around the table and say, "Okay, how can we apply these lessons to a particular church? How are we going to actually do these things? How do we move from just simply ideas to execution?" So I'm not going to tell you what the idea is. It's right there; it's only a few hundred words. It really is the nugget of this entire book. At the end of the day, I'm going to leave it to you and your team to find that idea and to apply it and apply it well within your context.

For years, I've been struck by the fact that most churches' mission and vision statements are the same. There's some version of *'reach people with the message of Jesus and see those people grow in their relationship with Jesus.'* If this is true (which is), then what's different about the churches that are prevailing?

It's not that those churches have a different mission because they don't.

It's not that the churches that are prevailing have a different vision because they don't.

It's not that the people who are working in those churches have some sort of special revelation because they don't. I really do believe that the same Holy Spirit that is active in me is active in you. Therefore, it can't be some sort of divine revelation.

It's not that God loves their church more than He loves your church because He loves His people.

He desperately wants to see your church make an impact.

So what is the difference between those churches that are beating the odds and seeing people come into the Kingdom on a regular basis, and those that are struggling to keep their doors open, or those that are simply flat-lined?

It all comes down to execution. The churches that make a difference have leaders who wake up on a Monday morning after church and ask the following questions:

- How can we do what we did yesterday again this coming week better than we did it last week?

- How do we reach more people through our ministry?

- How do we see more people connected with the teaching of Jesus than we've ever seen before?"

There's a consistent, dogged determination and discipline of execution within these churches. It really is a mindset that moves from between your ears to your hands and moves the people to engage in activities in a way that makes a difference.

My question for you, church leader, as you're reading through and leaning over the shoulder of other church leaders, is this: **Are you willing to apply what you're learning?**

Are you willing to not just read a book like this and put it up on a shelf, but are you willing to put those lessons into action?

I'm convinced that you wouldn't have read to this far in the book if you're not the kind of leader who has the kind of push-through and determination required to see these systems make a difference in the life of their churches. You see, most of the people can barely get past the first 10% of any book. If you make it to the last 10%, then you are within a radical minority of leaders. You have the determination to make a difference in your church.

God wants to do something amazing in your church. He wants to see more kids, more young adults, more adults, and more seniors connected to your ministry than ever before. I really do believe that if you apply these five aspects of the Church Growth Flywheel to your community, you'll witness amazing things happen.

Thank you so much for investing your time in reading this book. I'm super excited to see what God does in the life of your church. Please reach out. I'd love to hear how this book wrote a story in your church.

NOW WHAT? ARE YOU CAUGHT IN A PICKLE?

AS YOU JOURNEYED through this book, I'm sure it kept dawning on you that this is indeed a church communications book. At its core, the *Church Growth Flywheel* is about telling your story over and over again to your community so that it will spread like it needs to. It's about being remarkable - literally - so that people will remark about the great things happening at your church. I think there is one aspect of being "remarkable" that we didn't talk about much through the book but I think you need a plan for.

Studies have shown that 65 % of people are visual learners. This means that they prefer to take image messages as images, graphics, diagrams, etc. **If you are trying to communicate with your people and you don't have strong and consistently engaging**

visuals, then nearly 2/3rds of your people will simply tune you out! As we look at the fastest growing churches in the country, we can notice that all of them are unwaveringly committed to a great graphic design that has a penchant for expanding the attention span of the attendees.

But how can a church leader like you produce all the needed graphics that are required to communicate your message effectively?

Each aspect of the *Church Growth Flywheel* could be intensive from a design point of view. Think back over the 5 areas we talked about and before you know - the need for graphic design flashes on top of mind:

- **Big Days -** When you're in the month counting down to Easter or Christmas Eve, you need to increase the amount of graphics you produce, but are busy with lots of other details to make those events great!

- **Series Roll Outs -** In this chapter, we talked about the consistent communication that is required every time a new series launches. I've found that this requires 20-30 similar custom graphics every time a new series begins.

- **Social Media -** Regardless of what platform you use, people are always wanting of more visual content. Leading churches are producing custom graphics that are releasing multiple times a week, if not multiple times a day!

- **Community Engagement -** Mobilizing 70-80% of your people to get them out of their seats and into the streets requires all kinds of sign up forms, social media graphics & much more. These special events also generate a lot of images that need to be tweaked to share just after the event.

- **Internal Communication -** Previously, churches could just print a flyer on a different color paper in order to get people's attention. This just won't do any more! Each of your areas needs clear and compelling visuals that are "on brand" and move people to action.

How can you produce all these graphics and still manage to run a church?

It seems like we're in a pickle, caught between the needs of running your church and the importance of great graphics to communicate what's happening!

Luckily, the good people at Design Pickle are happy to help. **They have worked with hundreds of churches like yours to take care of all kinds of all your graphic design needs.** I've been so happy with them and I would love you to try their service.

Design Pickle is:

- **Flat-rate //** You pay just one super budget friendly low price to access their service. By paying a fraction of the cost of a part time graphic designer, you can access their services.

- **Always available //** If you can describe what you need in an email, then they are perfect for you. Just email their team and they will get working on it right away. Most times you'll get your finished designs back within 24 - 48 hours!

- **Ego-free //** They just want to help. They aren't hung up on what they want, but would like you to get them exactly what is most helpful.

- **Team friendly //** Already have a designer? No problem! Design Pickle is an extra dash of help, without the full-time salary. They are a big help to any overloaded creative team.

- **No risk //** Trying them out is 100% zero-risk proposition. You can work with the Design Pickle team and see if it's a fit. If so, great! If not, you get a full 100% refund without any hassle.

- **Unlimited graphic design help //** Seriously...you can send them as much as you need. We use them for everything at unSeminary!

Drop by DesignPickle.com and use the discount code *CHURCHGROWTH* to get 20% off on your first month.

I whole heartily endorse them. I really do think that every church that reads this book should give them a try. You'll find their service will help you in all kinds of ways and will find new and fun uses all the time!

Russ Perry, the founder of Design Pickle, is a great guy. He loves helping churches like yours. In fact, one of his first clients was a church that he attends in Scottsdale, Arizona. Helping churches has been at their core right from the beginning.

But don't just take my word for it...check out what these church leaders from prevailing churches have had to say about their experiences with Design Pickle:

"As a church, we are constantly needing designs for social media and print. We have a couple designers that work for us at times, but they are always too busy to deliver in a timely matter. We use Design Pickle because of the quick turnaround and unlimited design!"
- DAN SLAGLE, LEAD PASTOR, CHURCH:SD

"We use Design Pickle to help us relieve some of the creative production work we do as a church. I've found it helpful to pass them social media graphics, more tedious design work, and those extra projects when these get

busy around here! I'm thankful for the way Design Pickle has been able to relieve some of the pressure for us - allowing us to do more without breaking the bank."
- Justin Piercy, Service Programming Director, Connexus Church

What are you waiting for? All those compelling graphics aren't going to be made themselves!

Drop by DesignPickle.com, and use the code *CHURCHGROWTH* to save time and money.

Let me know if you try them out. I'd love to hear the types of projects you've found helpful to send to them. Drop me an email and let me know: rich@unseminary.com

NOW WHAT? YOU WOULDN'T BUILD A HOUSE? WOULD YOU?

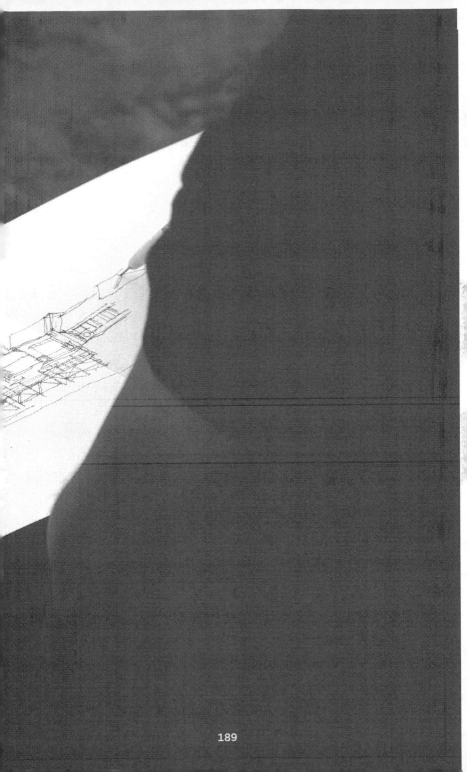

HAVE YOU EVER walked into a house that you absolutely love? You know the sort of place, the moment you walk in the front door it just feels amazing. My friend Andy's has a lake house that does that for me. **I wish you could see his place.** It has this great kitchen and family room combo space with a vaulted ceiling held up by exposed timber framing. To the front of the house are these massive floor-to-ceiling windows that look through the pine trees to the most majestic view of the lake you can imagine. It's the perfect blend of comfortable space with the great outdoors. When I arrive at his place I can literally feel myself slowing down and feeling more relaxed. Andy's place isn't fancy or ostentatious but it's elegant in its simplicity. I love it.

What about the most perfect house you've been to? What makes it special? What do you like about it? **What is it about that house that makes it so special?** Why do you love it?

Even if you've been in that place hundreds of time would you ever be crazy enough to try to build it? **Would you ever try to replicate what makes this house so special to you?** Would you know where to start with submitting the right drawing to the city to get approvals? How about the calculations required to ensure that that the roof holds up over time? What about something like knowing how the heating, air conditioning interacts with the plumbing and electrical?

Building a home is a complex undertaking.

Even though you can walk into a house and know right away you love that place most of us can't describe even the most basic processes that you have to go through to build it. **You require a series of architects, general contractors and subcontractors to take your idea all the way through to execution.** You need help to bring your vision into reality.

The same thing is true with seeing your church thrive and grow. You most likely are going to need help along the way. **This book is the beginning but you are going to need more support to see your vision of a thriving church come to full fruition.** In the same way that you need professionals with experience in order to help you build a house you'd love, you are going to need professionals with experience to help take your church to next level.

But don't worry. We're here to help.

Our motto at unSeminary is ALWAYS HELPING CHURCH LEADERS and we've put together a series of resources, coaching and support to take your church to next level. We want to be your guides as you see your church reach more people. Below are three ways we can help you take the lessons from this book and apply them in even a deeper manner in your church.

12 Insider Interviews with 12 of the Fastest Growing Churches

www.unseminary.com/12interviews

This FREE resource includes over 4.5 hours of interviews with church leaders from within the fastest growing churches in the country. Here from these leaders first hand on what makes their churches tick. Each day for 12 days a new interview is delivered to your inbox including summary notes that you can easily share with your team to extend the learning!

> "Invaluable stuff if you are serious about growing your church. **The resources are real world practical.**"
>
> – JOSH SCHOON, PASTOR

BONUS: By signing up for these FREE 12 insider interview you will also receive our weekly unSeminary resource emails that includes articles and podcasts to help your church grow even faster.

Church Growth Flywheel Insider Group Coaching

www.unseminary.com/growthgroup

Every month you and your team will be invited to a group coaching video call with me and possibly a guest or two. We'll cover one aspect of the Church Growth Flywheel with up to date examples, templates, interviews and more. This live experience also allows you to get your questions answered about that month's focus on church growth or anything else you're facing. Your church needs a growth coach and this is an ideal experience for churches of all sizes.

> "I've pastor a church in Hawaii for the past 16 years and wish I had your resource back then. It would have saved me a lot of mistakes! **Your equipping resources are some of the best I've found! You're a great communicator!**"
> – DAVE BARR, NEW HOPE CHURCH

SIGN UP NOW: You'll also receive access to all of our unSeminary premium online courses as well. This includes resources on big day planning, email marketing, volunteer management, guest connections and so much more.

Onsite Coaching with Rich Birch

www.unseminary.com/growthcoaching

I take on a limited number of senior leadership teams looking to do intensive on site coaching. One day a month for 6 months I'm on site at your location and deep dive into the Church Growth Flywheel and apply these lessons directly to your church. This "done with you" coaching experience is like me being on your team as we work through the particulars of seeing your church impact more people.

> "We love Rich Birch! Rich recently spent a weekend with our team at Grace Central Coach where he provided invaluable coaching for our outreach strategy. **He not only brought compelling research, but fantastic ideas that fit in our unique ministry context.** Our team was challenged and we are taking practical next steps in our vision to share the Gospel with the Central Coast of California and the next generation, thanks to Rich. We can't wait to have him out to Grace Central Coast again."
>
> – TIM THEULE, SENIOR PASTOR, GRACE CENTRAL COAST

SPACE IS LIMITED: As you can imagine, I can only take on a handful of onsite coaching client churches at any given time. This premium experience sells out quickly, but reach out today to see if we can find a time that works for your leadership team. You can drop by the web address right above or if you want to call me directly dial 201-882-4769

ACKNOWLEDGEMENTS

"Genuine thankfulness is an act of the heart's affections, not an act of the lips' muscles."
JOHN PIPER

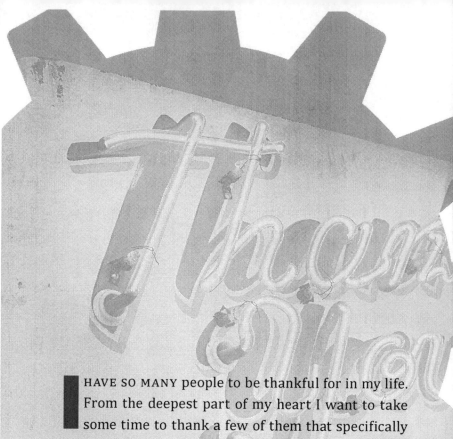

I HAVE SO MANY people to be thankful for in my life. From the deepest part of my heart I want to take some time to thank a few of them that specifically helped get this book out my head and into your hands. My name is on the front of this book but it really wouldn't have come together without these amazing people!

Christine, my dear wife. Your encouragement to get this book out the door motivated me to buckle down and get it done.

Haley, my daughter. I love the phase of life you're in right now. **It's a deep joy to see you "launching" into the next chapter of your life!**

Hunter, my son. Your passion for music and life is inspiring. You are growing into an honorable young man. I'm excited to see what adventures you take on in life.

Beth Colletti is the real reason anything actually ever happens at unSeminary. I love working on this stuff together with you!

Wow! **Carl George wrote the foreword!** What an incredibly generous and thoughtful leader! I'm so thankful that he went out of his way to encourage this project in such a practical way.

Charlotte Farley helped **transform these ideas with some structure and form.** I'm so thankful for our new friendship and I hope we work together in the future!

Russ Perry & the entire Design Pickle team have been cheerleaders of unSeminary for a few years. They do all of our graphic design work and you really should let them support your church. Check them out at **DesignPickle.com and use the discount code** *ChurchGrowth* to save.

Each of the **church leaders highlighted in this book are my heroes.** Thanks for letting us tell your stories! (Also to the 200+ church leaders we've interviewed on the unSeminary podcast - thank you for allowing me to learn from you!)

So much of this book comes out of my experience serving at Liquid Church in New Jersey. I'm thankful for the Lead Team I got to serve with at this amazing church. **Tim Lucas, Dave Brooks & Mike Leahy are some of the best teammates a person could ever ask for.**

I **love the interior book design that Steve Plummer did** (again!)…it looks so much more professional than it actually is.

Last but not least I want to thank the church leaders who invested energy in reading and applying the lessons from this book. We've chosen a tough career path that is fraught with all kinds of struggles and setbacks. The fact that you keep showing up every week to reach and serve people in your community inspires me. *Keep leaning in. The best is yet to come.*

Rich Birch
Winter 2018

ABOUT RICH

I'VE BEEN INVOLVED IN CHURCH LEADERSHIP FOR OVER 20 YEARS. EARLY ON I HAD THE PRIVILEGE OF LEADING IN ONE OF THE VERY FIRST MULTISITE CHURCHES IN NORTH AMERICA. I LED THE CHARGE IN HELPING THE MEETING HOUSE IN TORONTO TO BECOME THE LEADING MULTI-SITE CHURCH IN CANADA WITH OVER 4,500 PEOPLE IN 6 LOCATIONS. (TODAY THEY ARE 18 LOCATIONS WITH SOMEWHERE AROUND 6,000 PEOPLE ATTENDING.) IN ADDITION, I SERVED ON THE LEADERSHIP TEAM OF CONNEXUS COMMUNITY CHURCH IN ONTARIO, A NORTH POINT COMMUNITY CHURCH STRATEGIC PARTNER.

FOR SEVEN YEARS I SERVED AS A PART OF THE FOUR-MEMBER LEAD TEAM AT LIQUID CHURCH IN THE MANHATTAN FACING COMMUNITIES OF NEW JERSEY. IN MY TIME WITH THE CHURCH WE GREW FROM 1 CAMPUS TO 6 … AND OUR ATTENDANCE GREW TO OVER 3,500 PEOPLE. (THAT'S ACTUAL NUMBERS NOT "PASTOR INFLATED NUMBERS!") AT LIQUID I OVERSAW COMMUNICATIONS, WEEKEND SERVICE PROGRAMMING, CAMPUS EXPANSION AND SPECIAL PROJECTS.

I SPEAK AT CONFERENCES LIKE ORANGE, WFX AND VARIOUS REGIONAL MULTISITE CHURCH EVENTS. I'M A FEATURED WRITER ON AUXANO'S VISION ROOM, CHURCHLEADERS.COM AND MINISTRYBRIEFING.

I'M HONORED BLOG AND PODCAST WEEKLY AT UNSEMINARY.COM

I'M MARRIED TO CHRISTINE AND TOGETHER WE PARENT TWO WONDERFUL TEENS, HALEY AND HUNTER. COLLECTIVELY WE TRY TO KEEP OUR DOG, RORY, FROM CHEWING EVERYTHING THAT LANDS ON THE FLOOR.

PODCAST

**LISTEN WEEKLY FOR
MORE DISCUSSIONS
TO HELP YOUR
CHURCH REACH
MORE PEOPLE.**